NEW CASTLE, DELAWARE:
A WALK THROUGH TIME

NEW CASTLE, DELAWARE:
A WALK THROUGH TIME

With best wishes to Janet,

December 2011

BARBARA E. BENSON

&

CAROL E. HOFFECKER

Barbara E. Benson

Carol E. Hoffecker

Oak Knoll Press
2011

First Edition 2011

Published by
Oak Knoll Press
310 Delaware Street
New Castle, DE 19720, USA
www.oakknoll.com

ISBN: 978-1-58456-297-9
ISBN: 978-1-58456-296-2

Publishing Director: Laura Williams
Typesetting & Design: Höhne-Werner Design

Library of Congress Cataloging-in-Publication Data

Benson, Barbara E. (Barbara Ellen), 1943-
  New Castle, Delaware : a walk through time / Barbara E. Benson & Carol E.
Hoffecker. -- 1st ed.
       p. cm.
  Includes bibliographical references and index.
  Summary: "A history of the city of New Castle, Delaware, from its
settlement by the Dutch in 1609 through 2011. Examines the town's various
architectural styles and neighborhoods, giving the histories of important
houses and buildings. Illustrated throughout with maps, photographs, and
drawings"--Provided by publisher.
  ISBN 978-1-58456-297-9 (alk. paper) -- ISBN 978-1-58456-296-2 (alk. paper)
  1. New Castle (Del.)--History. 2. Historic buildings--Delaware--New
Castle. 3. Neighborhoods--Delaware--New Castle. I. Hoffecker, Carol E. II.
Title.
  F174.N5B46 2011
  975.1'1--dc23
                              2011038939

♾ Printed in the United States of America on acid-free paper meeting the requirements
of ANSI/NISO Z39.48-1992 (Permanence of Paper)

All who love New Castle, and those who read this book,
owe a great debt of gratitude to Robert and Joan Appleby.
They envisioned this book, inspired the authors,
assisted in the research, and provided its underwriting.

CONTENTS

ACKNOWLEDGMENTS

New Castle, Delaware: A Walk through Time has carried us many places and has enabled us to make many new acquaintances and to renew old friendships along the way. To a person, every resident of New Castle who encountered us displayed pride in their town, their home, and their organizations. We thank everyone who shared their knowledge, enthusiasm, and hospitality with us.

Many people welcomed us into their homes. Some of our visits were pre-arranged but others occurred serendipitously as we walked down a street, admiring a house, taking notes and even pictures. All exhibited love, pride, and knowledge of the unique historic character of their homes, businesses, or churches. We particularly want to thank the following for their tours and insights: Keith Adams, Robert and Joan Appleby, Joann DellAversano, Robert Fleck, Roderick and Geraldine Gillespie, Nancy Jodlbauer, James and Rita Meek, Michael Moskovis and Dorothy Selinger, Lillian Shue, Phyllis Stellard, and Carlo and Joann Viola.

Other individuals willingly shared information, insights, and documents with us, including Alexander Alvini, Richard and Barbara Cooch, Florence Davis, Robert Davis, Alison Freeth, James Gambacorta, Rev. John P. Klevence, Felice Jo Lambden, Sally Monigle, Wynne Mund, and Petty and Jim Travers. Mayor John F. Klingmeyer and city staff members Mikki DiEmidio and Kimberly Burgmuller not only provided access to historic city council minute books, they tracked down documents and photographs for us to use.

The amount of printed and visual materials on a town as old and interesting as New Castle is daunting, to say the least, but the staffs at libraries and archives throughout Delaware provided all of the documents, books, maps, and photographs we requested, as well as items unknown to us that they knew would be helpful. Our thanks begin with the staff of the New Castle Historical Society: Michael Connolly, Bruce Dalleo, and Susan Richman. They always welcomed us, clearing space and making time to share their collections. It is safe to say that without Mike Connolly this book would not have been possible.

In addition to the staff of the New Castle Historical Society, we owe a great debt to a large number of professionals at five other institutions. Researchers working on topics in Delaware history are fortunate to have such friendly professionals in charge of priceless collections: Jon M. Williams, Linda Gross, and Marsha Warrick at the Hagley Musuem and Library; Timothy D. Murray, L. Rebecca J. Melvin, and Shaun D. Mullen at Special Collections, Morris Library, University of Delaware; Randy Goss, Bruce Haase, and Margaret Rohmbauer of the Delaware Public Archives; Cindy Snyder and Brian Cannon, New Castle Court House Museum; and Michele Anstine, Antoinette Milej, Constance J. Cooper, Ellen Rendle, Edward Rici, and Jennifer Potts, Delaware Historical Society.

We thank Carlo Viola for fine photography; James Meek for new cartography; and Hilary Mohaupt, University of Delaware, and Vernell Bass at Technology Concierge for their computer skills. James Groff shared his knowledge of historical brick making, and Joanne Mattern walked us through the thorny path of Delaware's early public documents.

Finally, we acknowledge those who showed us the great kindness to read the manuscript and to provide us with substantive and editorial suggestions: Joan Appleby, Robert Appleby, Michael Connolly, Bruce Dalleo, Margaret Hassert, James L. Meek, Timothy Mullin, Wynne Mund, and Christine Quinn. Their efforts saved us from mistakes and gaffes large and small. What remains is our responsibility.

INTRODUCTION

New Castle is an extraordinary town, an early outpost of European explorers and settlers and a colonial capital beautifully situated on one of America's great rivers. In a compact space it provides an unusual richness of architecture that spans more than three centuries. Sometimes people say that New Castle is so beautiful because it is a town that time forgot, but that isn't exactly true. The town does have four museums that showcase fine examples of the exterior and interior architecture of buildings where you can learn about how people lived in the past, but the town itself is not a museum, nor is it a place that remains frozen in an earlier era.

New Castle has changed over time, so you cannot literally step back into its past. There is much you can no longer see, or smell, or hear. You cannot see the earliest small log houses or fort; you cannot see a busy waterfront full of wharves, warehouses, small craft workshops, stores, inns, or taverns; you cannot see the smokestacks of later industries. You cannot see horses, carriages, wagons, ships of all sizes, trains, or trolleys. You cannot hear the cacophony of sounds of the past, nor smell the odors all those activities generated, nor be caught up in the hustle and bustle of those bygone eras.

But with the conjuring trick of your mind's eye, you can perhaps imagine those earlier times as you read about New Castle's history and architecture, and walk through its streets looking at a town that has comfortably carried its past into the present. Today its residents live twenty-first century lives while continuing a now 350-year-old tradition of building, preserving, adapting, even removing and altering their world. The future, of course, remains unknown, but if the past is any guide, New Castle will continue to change, which is what will always make the town a beautiful, living entity that seeks to balance celebrating the past with moving forward with the times.

Modern aerial view of New Castle on the Delaware River. *(Courtesy of New Castle Historical Society)*

A BRIEF HISTORY
of NEW CASTLE

Colonial Rivalries

New Castle's origins lie in the competition among European nations for trade and settlement along the Delaware River. In 1609 Henry Hudson, an Englishman employed by the Dutch, discovered the Delaware Bay. In the years that followed, other Dutch sailors explored the bay and then journeyed further north up the Delaware River. They sailed among treacherous shoals and past a landscape of low-lying wetlands that melded into shallow waters close to shore, a habitat for muskrats, water fowl, and spawning fish. Then, rather suddenly, there came a bend in the river that on the western side revealed higher ground above a sandy shoreline. Dry land stood close to the river's natural channel and thus offered easy access to the shore. The Dutchmen called this sandy point Sandhoek. It was the future site of New Castle.

The Dutch claimed the Delaware Bay and River, or, as they called it, the South River, by right of discovery. They built a trading post called Fort Nassau on the eastern bank, at the place that is now Gloucester, New Jersey. Their principal focus, however, was on the North River, now known as the Hudson. It was at the mouth of that river that in 1624 the Dutch West India Company established its American headquarters in the town of New Amsterdam. In the next decade the Dutch concentrated their efforts on New

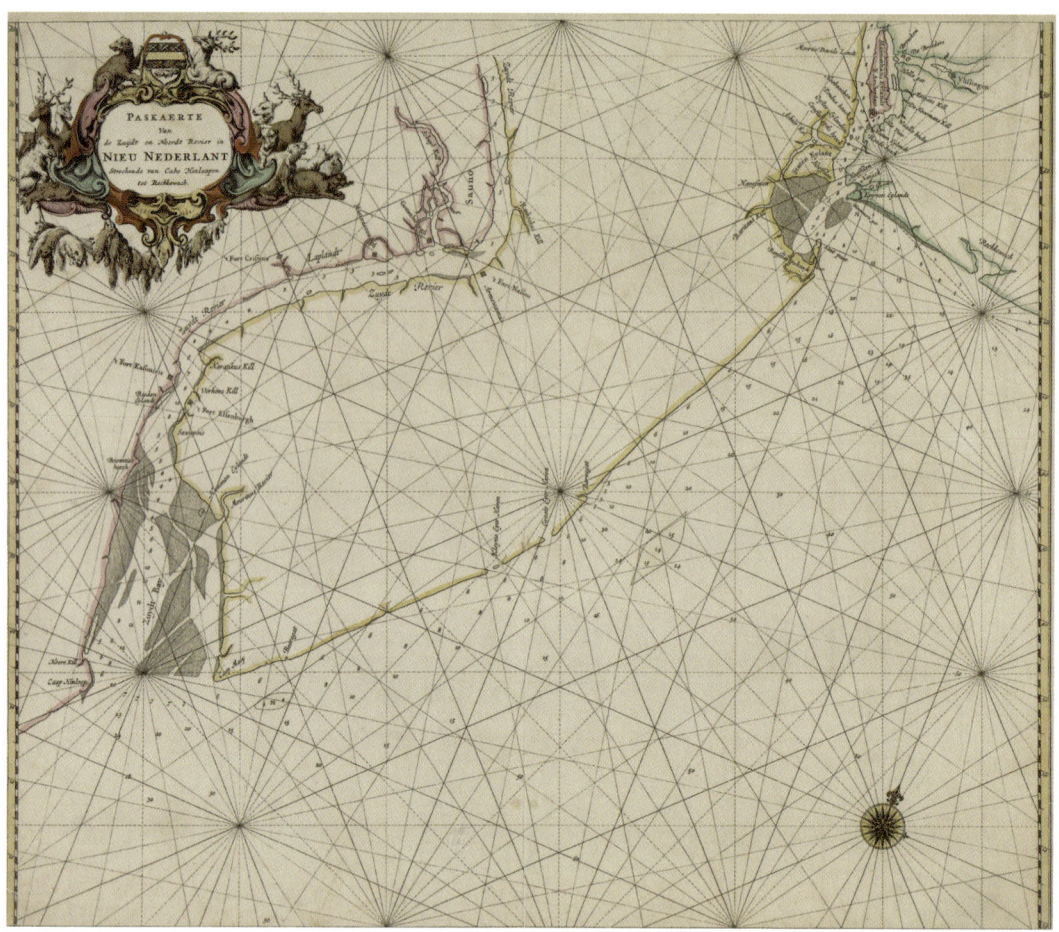

Early map of Dutch area of trade and settlement from the South, or Delaware, River to the North, or Hudson, River. New Castle took root at the location identified on the map as Fort Kalimiris. *(Courtesy of University of Delaware Library, Newark, Del.)*

Amsterdam and the North River. Sweden took advantage of the infrequent presence of Dutchmen on the South River, especially on its west side, to establish a colony of their own not far above the Sandhoek. In 1638, the Swedes purchased land from the Lenni Lenape Indians. The purchase included the point where two tributary rivers, the Christina and the Brandywine, join to flow into what we now call by the name later given by the English, the Delaware River. There the Swedes built a modest fort, called Fort Christina for their queen, and sent colonists from Sweden and Finland to establish farms along the river.

The main attraction of the Delaware River region to both colonial nations was not colonizing for its own sake, but rather the lucrative fur trade with the native people. The contest between the Dutch and Swedes to monopolize that trade provoked conflict. In 1647 the Dutch West India Company sent a new director-general named Peter Stuyvesant to New Amsterdam. An aggressive military man, he was determined to reclaim Dutch primacy on the Delaware River. On a reconnaissance sail up the river in 1651, Stuyvesant recognized the strategic importance of the Sandhoek, located as it was between the principal Swedish settlements and the sea, and decided to build a fort at the Sandhoek.

Stuyvesant negotiated the purchase of the land that now encompasses New Castle from local Lenni Lenape chiefs and commanded

Detail of Benjamin Ferris's *Map of the Original Settlements on the Delaware ...* with locations of Dutch and Swedish forts identified in red. *(Courtesy of Delaware Historical Society)*

the soldiers who had come with him to the Sandhoek to build a modest fort there. The Dutch fort consisted of a blockhouse built of logs, probably surrounded by a palisade and a trench, and equipped with cannons. Stuyvesant named it Fort Casimir to honor a Dutch nobleman and military hero. During the fort's construction Stuyvesant was called back to New Amsterdam to handle a serious Indian uprising. Thus, the fort was built quickly and rather shoddily.

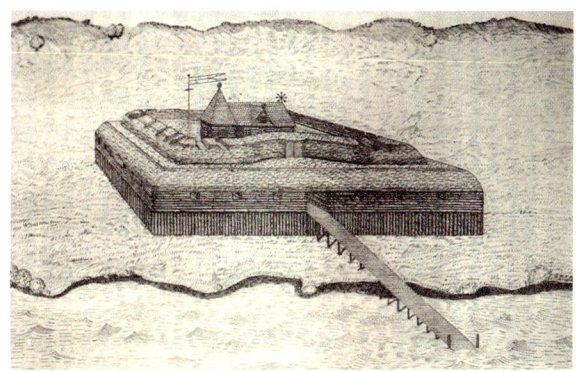

Over the years artists have attempted to interpret dimensionally the flat drawing made by Swedish engineer Peter Lindestrom of Fort Casimir after his restoration work in 1654-55. This attempt dates from 1905. *(Courtesy of Delaware Historical Society)*

Nothing of Fort Casimir can be seen above ground today, but late-twentieth-century archaeologists' discoveries suggest that the fort was located in the vicinity of Second and Chestnut streets. Modern visitors may think that location to be rather far from the river bank, but silt

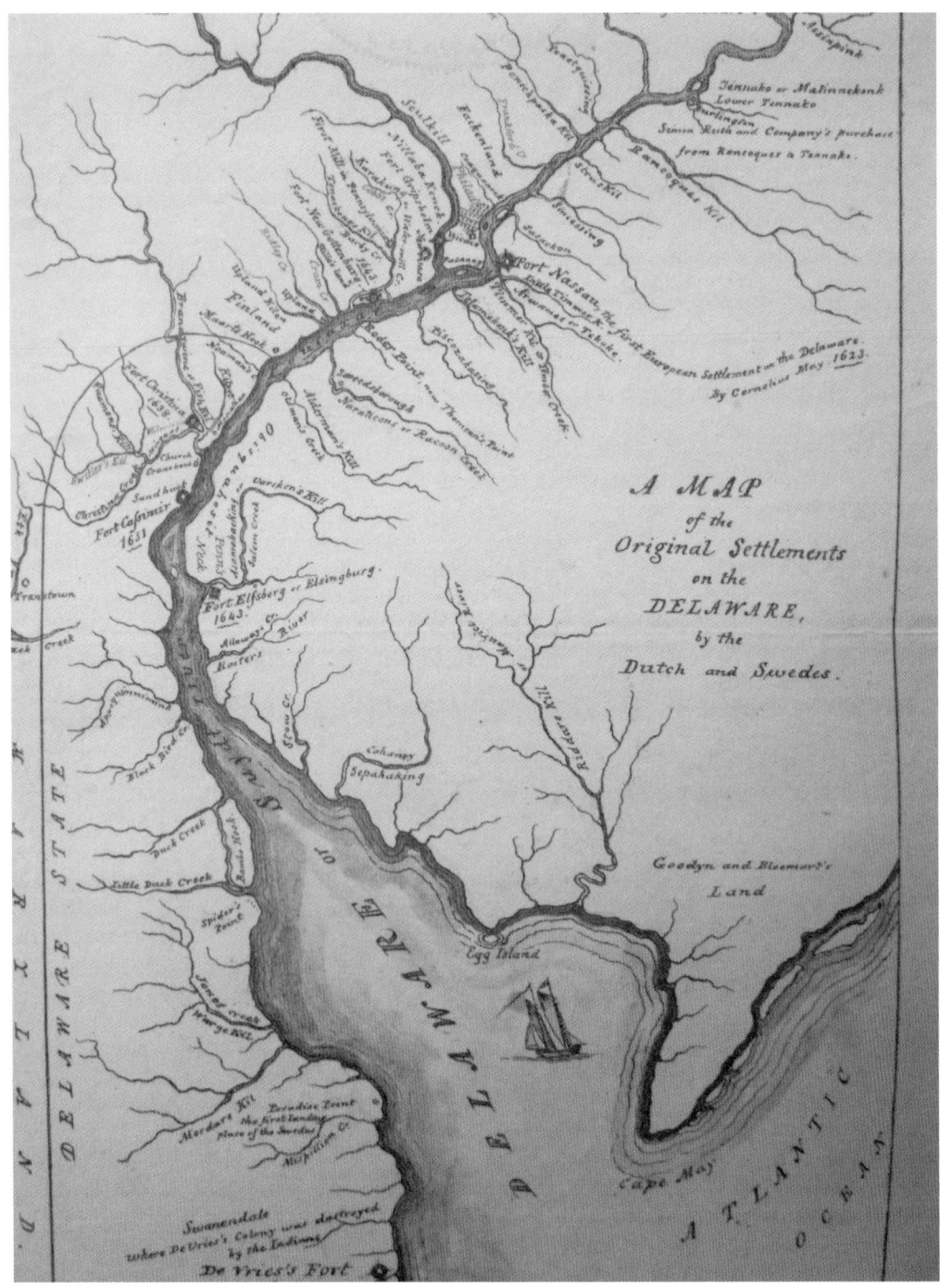

Full view of Ferris map, made for his book *Original Settlements on the Delaware,* published in 1845. *(Courtesy of Delaware Historical Society)*

has added about an extra block of dry land to the town since the seventeenth century.

Fort Casimir provided the impetus for the first European settlement of the immediate surrounding area. Next to the fort the Dutch built a village of small houses and shops. Like the fort, those buildings were constructed of wood, and all have vanished, but the footprint of the street they laid out (The Strand) remains in the present town. The first settlers came from Fort Nassau, New Amsterdam, and other parts of New Netherland. Over time small numbers of other Europeans seeking new opportunities

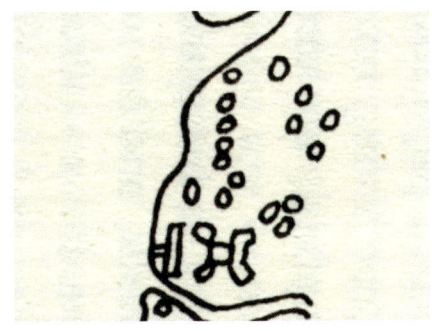

The earliest known view of the settlement that became New Castle is a detail of a map made by Swedish engineer Peter Lindestrom in 1654-55, and later copied by J.J. Alexander, showing the location of the fort and the sixteen houses built south of the fort. Reprinted in C.A. Weslager, *The Swedes and Dutch at New Castle* (Wilmington: Middle Atlantic Press, 1987)

or religious freedom came to the Dutch settlement on the Delaware. Though they were immigrants of different nationalities, the inhabitants got along together and generally experienced no serious problems with the Indians, who often came to town to trade skins for manufactured goods.

The leaders of the colonial governments of the competing European nations were less prone to peaceful relations than were the multi-national residents at Fort Casimir. On Trinity Sunday in 1654 the Swedes successfully attacked and captured the unmanned Fort Casimir, and renamed it Fort Trinity. A year later, Peter Stuyvesant returned with a flotilla of ships and retook the fort. New Sweden was his next objective, and that small, poorly defended colony fell to the Dutch in 1655. The Hollanders now controlled the entire South River and its trade with the native people. With peace secured under the aegis of one nation, the town at Sandhoek saw a growth in trade with ships coming from Holland, from New Amsterdam, and from other Dutch colonies, yet it remained a minor outpost of the Dutch empire.

During its early years the village adjacent to Fort Casimir grew to include a school, a horse-powered gristmill, and a small brick kiln capable of supplying bricks for fireplaces and chimneys. Property near the fort was designated to be the "Market Plaine" where farmers, shippers, and townspeople could

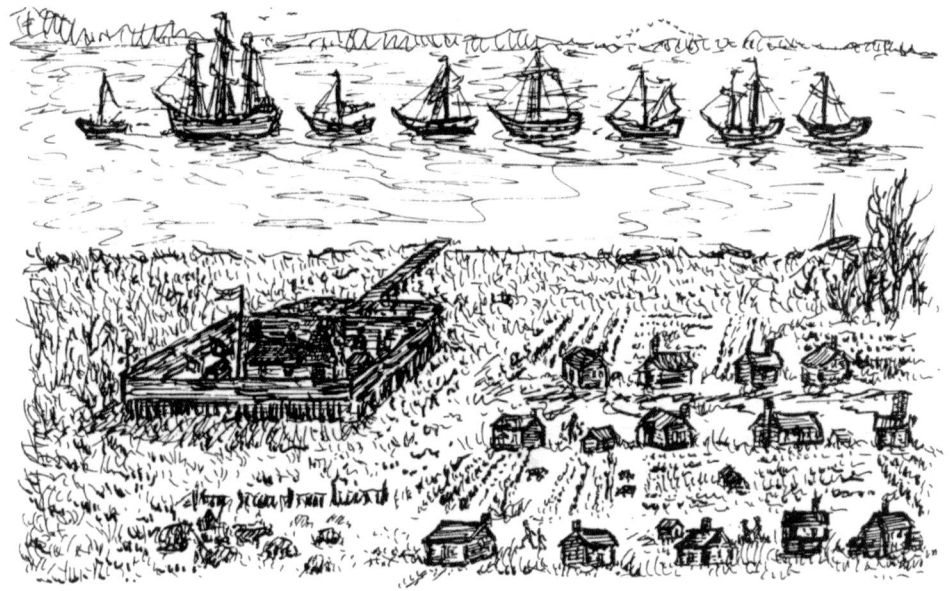

Delaware artist Nancy Sawin created this sketch of the town and Fort Casimir for C.A. Weslager's *New Sweden on the Delaware.* (Wilmington: Middle Atlantic Press, 1988)

negotiate the sale of their goods. The Dutch government at New Amsterdam established a court at their outpost on the South River. A *schout*, or as the English would say, sheriff, was appointed to enforce the laws, and the court met in the fort to resolve civil and criminal cases. Thus the town began its long history as a center of law and government.

The marshy landscape along the lower Delaware River was a terrain familiar to the Dutch, not unlike their low-lying, flood-prone lands at home, so it was natural for them to build earthen dikes near Fort Casimir to hold back the water of the river and to drain marshland. They established a land connection to the Swedish settlement on the Christina River by building a dike over marshland north of the fort to form the platform of a roadway. Farms were established nearby that provided grain, vegetables, and animals to feed the residents, as well as some tobacco for local consumption and for trade. Farm produce was sold in the village. In the years of Dutch rule, the fort served as the storehouse for imported goods and for goods awaiting export shipment.

In 1656 the City of Amsterdam took control of the settlement on the South River and renamed it New Amstel to honor the river that flows through the

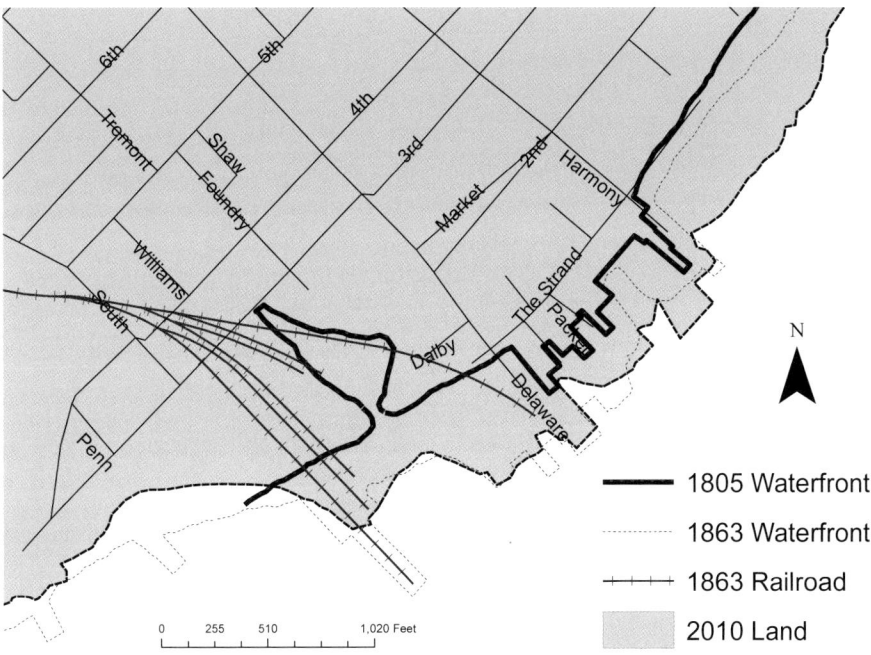

Map of changes to New Castle's shoreline over time created by James L. Meek for the website of the New Castle Center for Historic Architecture Project. *(Courtesy of James L. Meek)*

Dutch capital of Amsterdam. This arrangement is unique in the colonial history of the United States. Never before or since did a city own an American colony. The city took its ownership seriously and sent over several shiploads of settlers. Some of the new arrivals settled in the town, while others took up farming nearby. By then the fur trade was nearly exhausted, and tobacco had become the major cash producer, especially in the English colonies along the Chesapeake Bay of Virginia and nearby Maryland. A road was laid out to link New Amstel to Maryland, and the Dutch seized upon the opportunity to import enslaved Africans to New Amstel: some to be sold to the English in Maryland; a few to serve in the Dutch colony. Slaves, tobacco, and beer-making helped to make the small colony less dependent.

Meanwhile, across the ocean England was looking to expand its empire in North America by connecting its Chesapeake and New England colonies at the expense of their rivals in trade and colonization, the Dutch. Toward that end, King Charles II granted to his brother, James, Duke of York and Albany, lands that became the states of New York and New Jersey. James, in his capacity as Lord High Admiral of the English Navy, had but to send his navy to America to take them. In 1664 the duke's fleet, consisting of four warships led by Colonel Richard Nicholls, seized New Amsterdam from an angry but powerless Peter Stuyvesant and renamed it New York.

Although the Dutch colony on the west bank of the Delaware River had not been included in the duke's grant, Nicholls did not hesitate to send two of his ships under the command of Sir Robert Carr to capture New Amstel. When the Dutch offered resistance, the English landed troops just downstream from the fort. The soldiers marched to Fort Casimir's lightly defended land side and stormed the barricade. Three Dutch soldiers were killed and ten were wounded in the assault.

The Delaware River Valley, indeed the entire east coast of North America from the future state of Maine to that of Georgia, was now controlled by the English. One age of colonization had ended; another was coming into being. A simple, but not incorrect, way to imagine what had happened along the west bank of the Delaware River is to envision the well-known image of the small fish being eaten by the medium-sized fish, who is then consumed by the big fish. Now substitute New Sweden, New Netherland, and finally Britain's American colonies.

The absence of a title from the king to the west bank of the Delaware River did not inconvenience the duke or his representatives in America. It may, however, help account for the decision in 1665 to adopt the name of New Castle for the village. In that same year King Charles promoted William Cavendish, Earl of Newcastle, to become Duke of Newcastle. The name "New Castle" would most certainly have won the king's approval and may have eased Charles's acceptance of his brother's extension of his proprietorship to include the Delaware property.

The Duke of York's proprietorship lasted from 1664 until 1682, except for a brief interruption in 1673-74 when the Dutch retook the town during yet another conflict with the English. Under the duke's control, New Castle was the largest of the few small settlements on the Delaware River. The duke's government inherited a village of several hundred people, who were, regardless of nationality, encouraged to retain their homes and lands. Their magistrates and basic form of government were also carried forward, subject to oversight from the duke's government in New York and the introduction of English law. In 1672 New Castle became a *balywick* to be governed by a *bayley*, or bailiff, appointed from New York, along with six assistants to be elected by the townsmen. Thus began the first glimmer of democracy in what had hitherto been a series of autocratic colonial administrations.

Under the duke's government, New Castle's residents were largely left to manage their own affairs, subject to infrequent oversight from New York, but they lost the right to engage in direct trade to and from across the seas. Trade now focused on New York, where all cross-Atlantic ships were required to dock. New Castle was reduced to being the larger colony's subsidiary. Imported goods had to come via New York, and all crops, skins, and tobacco had to be sent to New York for export. Street names of that period such as Beaver, Otter, and Hay bear witness to New Castle's economic base.

The town's settlers and visitors included people of various religions and ethnicities, particularly Dutch Calvin-

WHAT'S IN A NAME

In the year 1080, fourteen years after William the Conqueror had sailed from Normandy to seize control of England, his son, known as Robert Cuthose, built a wooden fort on the River Tyne in northeastern England. His fort, like the Roman Wall, which had its eastern terminus nearby, was intended to protect against the Scots. A century later the crumbling fort was replaced by a new castle constructed of stone. The town that grew up around the fortification was thus called Newcastle-on-Tyne. As the principal harbor in an area that later came to be dominated by collieries, the English language gained the expression "to bring coals to Newcastle," which means to bring a commodity to a place that already has it in abundance.

William Cavendish, the first Duke of Newcastle (1593-1676) was a courtier who served as tutor to Prince Charles, later King Charles II. Cavendish taught the prince to be a gentleman, gracious to the ladies, a good horseman, and a capable politician and warrior. Learning from books was not emphasized. The prince took to this approach and learned his lessons well.

The English spell the town and the noble title as one word: *Newcastle*. In America it became two words: *New Castle*.

ists, Swedish and Finnish Lutherans, and English Anglicans, as well as a few Roman Catholics and at least one Jew. Despite or perhaps because of its diversity, the merchants and tradesmen who made up the town got along well together and experienced little crime or disharmony.

During the Duke of York years the town's population continued to vary depending upon economic conditions. The loss of cross-oceanic trade ensured that the town never reached the significance it had achieved by the end of the Dutch period. Although New Castle's appearance changed little, there were some signs of development. A church, now lost, was built, and the market square became more defined. In the 1670s the decaying Fort Casimir was replaced by a new wooden blockhouse that was constructed near the market on land that is now occupied by Immanuel Church to serve as both a military and administrative headquarters. The blockhouse held a few small cannon, a jail, and offices. It was the place where the court met to decide cases not only involving New Castle residents, but also disputes and crimes coming out of the surrounding countryside. In other words, this period saw

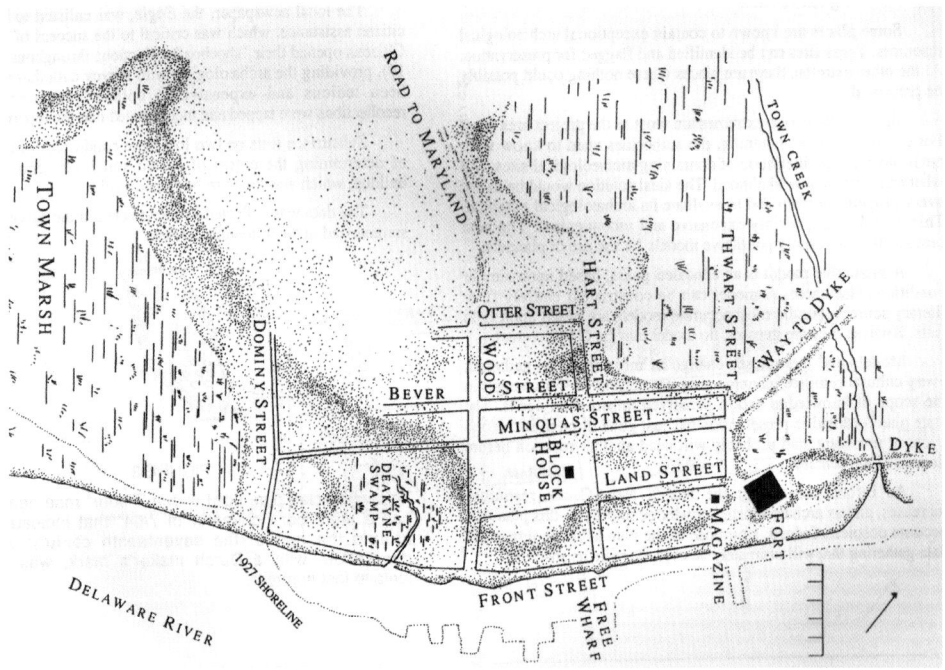

Map of New Amstel townsite, drawn by Louise Heite for her thesis, "New Castle under the Duke of York … ," University of Delaware, 1978. *(Courtesy of New Castle Historical Society)*

the beginnings of New Castle County and made the town a county seat. In the Duke of York years, New Castle lost some of its commercial significance, but it was becoming a government center. That development set the stage for the town's future.

The Penn Period

No event in New Castle's history is more famous than the ceremony that took place on October 27, 1682, when the Duke of York's magistrates transferred the colony to William Penn. The event marked a major turning point, not only for the town, but also for the creation of the State of Delaware.

William Penn was an aristocrat by birth, the son of an English admiral. At twenty-three he rejected his family's Anglican faith and warrior heritage to embrace the Quaker religion, which emphasized peaceful relations and social equality. When the admiral died, Penn inherited a substantial debt that King Charles II owed to his deceased father. Rather than demand money, in 1680 William Penn asked for a grant of land in America to establish a refuge for the persecuted Quakers. That grant is now the State of Pennsylvania.

At first, seeing Pennsylvania's proximity to his New Castle colony down river, the duke and his representatives were apprehensive about the Delaware colony's future. To assuage those fears, it was decided in London to draw a twelve-mile circle from New Castle to protect the duke's colony from encroachment by Penn's colony. The survey was made from the top of the broad dike adjacent to the town, which is now commemorated by a marker at the intersection of Third and Chestnut streets. Subsequently, in 1752, the twelve-mile circle was resurveyed from the courthouse in New Castle, but in 1681 that building had not as yet been built.

The king's large gift of real estate to William Penn offered everything a proprietor could wish for, with one exception: the Province of Pennsylvania lacked direct access to the sea. To get that, Penn needed the Duke of York's colony on the Delaware River and Bay. Fortunately for Penn, the duke was his friend and was amenable to the Quaker proprietor's request. Thus, the king's brother transferred his three counties along the west bank of the river and bay to Penn. The new Quaker owner called the three counties, each with its own court, the Three Lower Counties on Delaware. Those counties now constitute the State of Delaware.

When Penn and scores of Quaker settlers bound for Pennsylvania arrived at New Castle on October 27, 1682, aboard the ship *Welcome,* the new owner of the colony was himself welcomed. Escorted by cheering townspeople to the blockhouse, he was given its key and was also presented with a twig, soil, and river water to symbolize his ownership. The day of the isolated frontier settlement was about to end. A new era in New Castle's history as part of an expanding, commercially energized colony was about to begin.

Symbolically one of the first changes was the proprietor's official designation of the Market Square, or Green, as a public place. This central square had served that need since the Dutch settlement. The New Castle Green was a place for farmers to sell their produce and for other public purposes. Penn removed the militaristic blockhouse and in 1687 built New Castle County's first courthouse and jail on the public Green facing present-day Delaware Street. The original courthouse was constructed of wood. When that building burned in 1729, it was replaced by the brick courthouse, completed in 1732, that stands today. Now a state museum, the colonial New Castle Courthouse is Delaware's oldest surviving government building.

The transfer of ownership of the Three Lower Counties from the Duke of York to William Penn had a profound effect on every aspect of life in New Castle and the surrounding region. Penn introduced representative government into his

Statue of William Penn by Charles Parks, created to commemorate the Quaker proprietor's landing in 1682. All of the symbols of his ownership of the colony are held in his hands.

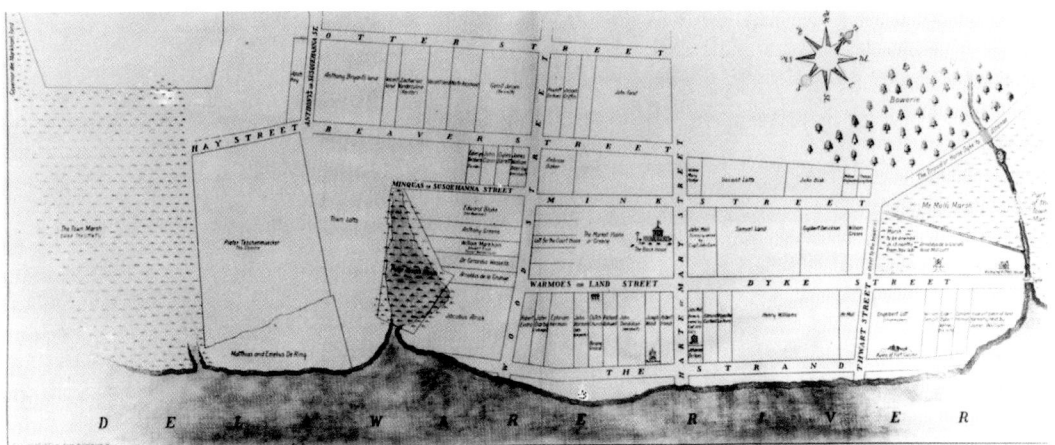

Long-time State Archivist Leon deValinger created this map to show the town's size at the time of New Castle's 250th anniversary in 1932. *(Courtesy of Delaware Public Archives)*

colonies; he encouraged immigration, especially by religious dissenters; and he laid out a city upstream on the Delaware River in Pennsylvania, which he named Philadelphia. His new city quickly eclipsed New Castle to become the principal place of government and commerce in the Delaware Valley.

The proprietor was eager to meld his two grants of land into a unified, harmonious whole. Toward that end, he divided Pennsylvania into three counties to match the three lower counties of the duke's grant. He then introduced a legislative body called the General Assembly to be composed of an equal number of members from each of the six counties. The Assembly met annually, usually in Philadelphia, but on three occasions, in 1684, 1690, and 1700, it met in New Castle. Penn's attempt to ensure equality worked for a while, but in time there was friction as the population of Pennsylvania increased much more rapidly than did that of the Lower Counties. An additional point of contention concerned the issue of defense. The Quakers who dominated Pennsylvania's politics refused to provide the Lower Counties with the protection they needed to thwart raids by pirates and other hostile vessels that from time to time sailed into the bay and river. Sometimes those hostile vessels sailed as far up river as New Castle, but they never sailed so far as Philadelphia.

Forced to acknowledge the dissension between legislators from his two colonies, Penn reluctantly agreed to the creation of two separate assemblies to serve under a common governor. The General Assembly of the Delaware colony met for the first time in 1704 in the New Castle Courthouse, which was to be its home for the remainder of the colonial period. New Castle, then the largest town in the Delaware colony, was now its official capital.

But William Penn never got to meet with the Delaware colony's assembly. Barely twenty years into his proprietorship, he faced bankruptcy and a serious legal challenge to his claim to the Delaware colony from the Calvert family, the proprietors of Maryland. Reluctantly, Penn set sail for England to press his case in court. In 1701 when his ship cast anchor from New Castle, Penn left his American colonies, never to return. He did not live long enough to see the English court uphold the Penn family's rights to Delaware or to witness the work of the surveyors Charles Mason and Jeremiah Dixon, who established the border that separated the Penn family's colonies of Pennsylvania and Delaware from the Calvert family's Maryland in the 1760s.

Looking around New Castle some three hundred years later, residents or visitors are likely to imagine that what they are seeing is not unlike what William Penn saw in his last view of the town. That image, however, would be quite wrong. Where he saw a town almost exclusively of wood, we see a town of brick. Where he saw a landscape of uneven ground—some places marshland, other places slightly hilly—we see ground that has been leveled. The only similarities remaining from that time are the earthen dikes on New Castle's up-river side, and the street pattern. All else is post 1701.

Soon after Penn's departure, New Castle began to undergo significant changes. A drainage project completed in 1717 began to push back the

Immanuel Episcopal Church, built in 1703, from the Latrobe Survey of 1804-05. *(Courtesy of Delaware Public Archives)*

marshes that had nearly surrounded the town's land sides. A brickyard was established that permitted the erection of more durable structures, some of which have become hallmarks of the town. Churches led the way, beginning with Immanuel Episcopal Church, built on the Green in 1703. Why a church on common land? William Penn dared not offend the Church of England while he fought for his colony in an English court. This favoritism riled the Calvinists, that is, the Dutch Reformed and the Scots-Irish Presbyterians, who built their church across from the Green alongside the market stalls in 1707. Both the Episcopal and Presbyterian churches still stand today.

The years from Penn's departure from America to the Revolutionary War were marked by growth in the population, economy, and legal life of New Castle County that greatly influenced developments in the county seat. Farms, villages, and new towns filled much of the landscape. The colony's openness to members of dissenting faiths and its proximity to Philadelphia encouraged the settlement of Quaker farmers, merchants, and artisans throughout the county, but principally in the commercial town of Wilmington. That town was established in the 1730s near the site of the former Swedish settlement where the Brandywine, Christina, and Delaware rivers meet.

The Quakers built a Meeting House in New Castle in 1705, but their faith did not grow in the town. In 1758 the Wilmington Meeting decided to consolidate New Castle's few Quakers into their much larger meeting, and this was accomplished by 1763. The Quaker Meeting House located at Fourth and Williams streets in New Castle later served as a school, church, and home before it was demolished in 1885. It is now the location of the Good-Will Fire Company.

Wilmington and New Castle were rivals. Wilmington lacked New Castle's advantage of location directly on the Delaware River, but the new town offered other advantages that New Castle could not emulate. The rapid-flowing Brandywine River came down from hills to reach tidewater at Brandywine Village, a hamlet adjacent to Wilmington. There the descending river provided the power to turn the waterwheels that ground the flour that was fast becoming the county's major export. The Christina River, which flowed beside Wilmington's harbor, was navigable from the Delaware River into

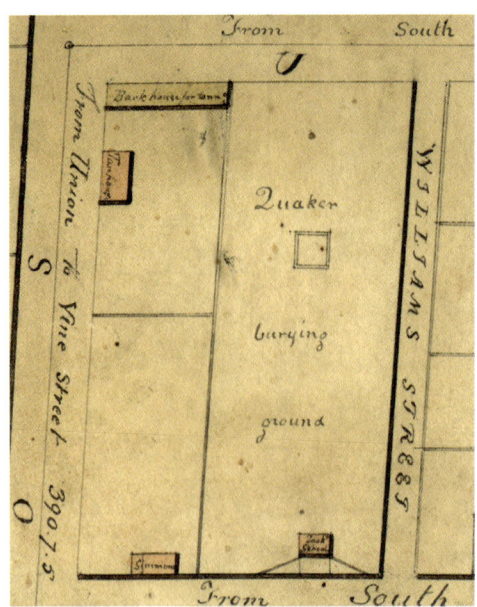

Quaker burying ground on Williams Street between today's West Fourth and West Fifth streets, from the Latrobe Survey. *(Courtesy of Delaware Public Archives)*

the farms and villages that were transforming New Castle County. Along the Christina's formerly quiet banks could be heard the sound of ships being built to be sent to trade with the West Indies and the mother country.

New Castle did not have those natural advantages. Its merchants could not compete with those of Philadelphia in the lucrative flour trade as could those of the upstart town of Wilmington. But New Castle did possess one asset that Wilmington did not have: the ownership of over a thousand acres of land adjacent to the town. This extensive property, called the New Castle Common, derived from the Dutch period. The Common received its unimpeachable legal status from William Penn, who ordered the survey of the land's extent in 1704. In 1764 Delaware's Assembly transferred administration of the land to an elected board called the Trustees of the Common, a body that still exists today. The trustees determine the use of the land, collect rent from its occupants, and use that money to assist the town and its environs in the interests of the community. For almost 250 years their largesse has kept New Castle's services high and its taxes low.

During Penn's proprietorship, New Castle was a major port of entry for immigrants to America, especially for ships that brought a deluge of newcomers from Northern Ireland called the Scots-Irish. Those Presbyterian Scotsmen, whose ancestors had moved to Ireland in the early 1600s, sought new opportunities in America away from the religious and economic restrictions being imposed on them at home by the English government. The flood of Scots-Irish began coming to the Delaware Valley in about 1715. Many of them first set foot on American soil at the port of New Castle. A few stayed or moved to nearby parts of the county. Most, however, set out for new homes in Pennsylvania or traveled on to the Shenandoah Valley and down into the Carolinas.

The migration greatly enhanced New Castle's trade and provided a steady stream of clients for the town's innkeepers. Inns and taverns were especially prominent on the street closest to the river, now called The Strand, which was the place where sailors and passengers embarked for, or disembarked from, lengthy sea voyages. New Castle was also an important market town for local farmers, who provided the provisions for those ships. In addition,

TRUSTEES OF THE COMMON

According to the jurist and historian, Judge Richard S. Rodney, the designation of common land for use by the residents of New Castle dates back to the period of Dutch rule. After a century of people cutting down trees and using the land with no thought for a common benefit, the town's leading men decided that a way must be found to maintain the land for the use of future generations. In 1760 they filed a petition with the Penn proprietors, and in 1764 Thomas and Richard Penn granted that request by creating the Trustees of the Common. There were to be thirteen trustees, who were appointed under the law and were to serve for life, now reduced to a term. When a term ends, the outgoing trustee is replaced by someone elected by the voters of New Castle for a twelve-year term. Although trustees no longer serve for life, they can continue to seek reelection.

The mandate of the trustees was to ensure that the common land was used for the benefit of the people of New Castle. They and their successors have been unerringly true to that civic responsibility. In the early days of the trusteeship, the common land was subdivided into tenant farms. The income from the rents was used to pay for improvements in the town such as streetlights, trees on the Green, a town clock, a wharf, better water supply, and cobblestone streets. The trustees also used common land profits to build the Academy and the Town Hall, and to buy the town's first fire engine. All of these improvements came without costing townspeople a penny in taxes. Indeed, there was no town tax in New Castle until 1850.

In 1885 a state law gave the trustees authority to sell parcels of common land and to invest the proceeds in sound investments. It was this provision that permitted the trustees to sell some land to steel corporations to entice them to relocate at New Castle. When the United States entered World War II, the trustees gave up land to create the New Castle Army Air Base. That land is now the New Castle County Airport and Delaware Air National Guard headquarters.

Perhaps the most important way in which the Trustees of the Common have served the people of New Castle in more recent times is their role, beginning in 1939, in the purchase and improvement of Battery Park. In response to that effort, the city of New Castle expanded the trustees' responsibilities to make them the city's Park Board.

the town's artisans made a variety of items such as bricks, beer, and barrels for residents, tradesmen, and those passing through the town.

New Castle was also a center of government. It served as both the seat of the court in a fast-growing county and the home of government for the Delaware colony. Every year the Assembly met in October, bringing eighteen legislators, six from each county, to the town to make the laws. The governor, who was sometimes a son of William Penn and sometimes an administrator hired by the Penns, traveled down from his headquarters in Philadelphia to attend the session. The legislative session began with the governor's address to the assemblymen. He then interacted with them about pending legislation and finally placed the Penn family seal on those laws that he approved. While in New Castle, the governor stayed at the town's best inn, the Indian King, located on The Strand across the street from Packet Alley, run by Judge Jehu Curtis and then his daughter and son-in-law, Anne and Slaytor Clay.

In 1706 England was engaged in one of the nation's intermittent wars with France, this one known as Queen Anne's War. Freed from the control of Pennsylvania's anti-war Quaker majority, the Delaware Assembly voted to construct a defensive battery supported by a few cannon on the down-river side of the town. Its purpose was to stop French privateers from sailing up the Delaware River to attack New Castle and the towns further up the river. It is now called Battery Park, but the cannons are gone.

By the middle of the eighteenth century New Castle had become an important port town and colonial capital. Its increasing population and economic development, together with the introduction of English law and legal procedures, attracted lawyers to live and work in New Castle. Indeed, lawyers occupied several of the most admired houses in the town's historic center, and New Castle remained a popular residence for lawyers and judges.

Two of the most important New Castle lawyers in the late colonial period were George Read and Thomas McKean. They had much in common. Both played leading roles in the Assembly and in the Revolutionary War. Both men's signatures are on the Declaration of Independence and the United States Constitution.

Read was the son of an Irish-born Maryland farmer. Recognizing his son's intellectual ability, the elder Read sent young George to New London, Pennsylvania, a hamlet very near the border with Delaware, to study at the newly established academy of a Scots-Irish Presbyterian minister named Francis Alison. Thomas McKean, whose father was a Scots-Irish tavern keeper, was also a student at that academy. Alison's school later moved across the border to nearby Newark, Delaware, and became the precursor to the University of Delaware.

Read and McKean went on to read law: Read in Philadelphia; McKean in the office of his New Castle relative, David Finney. Admitted to the bar in the same year of 1754, they settled in New Castle, worked hard to gain clients and recognition, and then entered politics. They attended different churches: Read was an Anglican; McKean was a Presbyterian. Both were members of the Assembly when the British Parliament adopted the Stamp Act to tax Americans in 1765. Their training in the law prepared them to take the lead among their fellow assemblymen and citizens in protesting that law and subsequent British laws designed to tax the colonists as "taxation without representation."

Portrait of George Read. *(Courtesy of Delaware Historical Society)*

Portrait of Thomas McKean. *(Courtesy of Delaware Historical Society)*

Together with Caesar Rodney, the Assembly's speaker from Kent County, McKean was elected by his fellow assemblymen to represent Delaware at the Stamp Act Congress in Philadelphia. Both McKean and George Read later served Delaware in the first and second Continental Congresses. George Read was a determined leader of protests against British policies, but, when the Declaration of Independence was presented to the Congress, he was reluctant to break with the mother country before the new nation could get organized. McKean, however, having no such reluctance, sent a message to Caesar Rodney, then in Delaware, to hasten to Philadelphia to insure Delaware a majority vote for the Declaration. Rodney's overnight ride of July 1 and 2, 1776, which took him through New Castle, is now celebrated as the most famous event in Delaware's history. Recognizing that he was outvoted and had been perhaps overly cautious, Read also signed the document.

Thomas McKean eventually left New Castle and Delaware's politics for the larger world of Philadelphia, where he rose to become Chief Justice of Pennsylvania. George Read remained in New Castle. He represented Delaware at the Constitutional Convention and was chosen to be one of Delaware's first United States senators. His house on The Strand burned in the fire of 1824.

From the American Revolution to the Transportation Revolution

The American Revolution had a powerful effect on New Castle. In May 1776 two English warships bristling with guns, the HMS *Roebuck* and the HMS *Liverpool*, came up the Delaware River past the town and sailed as far as the Christina River. A flotilla of American galleys, one of which was commanded by George Read's brother, Thomas, came down the river from their base just below Philadelphia to engage them. The battle that followed took place over two days and could be both heard and observed from New Castle. Neither side scored a complete victory, but the British failed to lure the American galleys down-stream into the wider channel below New Castle where their larger vessels could maneuver to advantage. After the *Roebuck* was briefly stuck in muddy shallow water, the English ships retreated rather than risk getting grounded in the face of the Americans' cannon and fireboats.

Meanwhile, the Delaware Assembly continued its annual meetings in the New Castle Courthouse/Statehouse. A month after the battle on the river, on June 15, 1776, the Assembly adopted a bill proposed by the Second Continental Congress to separate from Great Britain. This event is still celebrated in New Castle as Separation Day. Likewise, on July 24, 1776, a gathering of 400 to 500, including New Castle residents and people from around the county, came to town to hear the Declaration of Independence read from the Courthouse. The crowd cheered and burned an image of the king's coat of arms.

As an independent state, no longer under the sovereignty of the king or the Penn family, Delaware held a constitutional convention to provide for a new state government. The convention met in New Castle, and George Read played a leading role in creating the new document. Another New Castle lawyer, Nicholas Van Dyke, was elected to represent Delaware in the Continental Congress in 1777. Van Dyke also helped write the state's first constitution and was elected Delaware's chief executive, then called the "president," in 1783.

In October 1776 the first General Assembly met under the new state constitution. All subsequent General Assembly sessions are dated from that meeting. The Assembly met where its predecessor colonial assemblies had convened, in the New Castle Courthouse. New Castle's role as the state's capital did not last long. As early as 1774, Dr. Charles Ridgely, a Dover politician, had demanded the removal of the assembly to his home town on the grounds that it was more centrally located in the state. New Castle's vulnerability to enemy naval attacks also argued in favor of the inland town in Kent County. The assemblymen from Kent and Sussex counties exercised their majority and voted to move Delaware's capital to Dover. The General Assembly held its final meeting in New Castle during the first week of June 1777.

The year 1777 proved to be the most dangerous of the war for people living in New Castle County. In late summer a large fleet brought 15,000 British and Hessian soldiers under the command of Sir William Howe from their base in New York to the upper reaches of the Chesapeake Bay. After land-

Delaware's elected representatives met in the Assembly Room on the second floor of the Courthouse through the evolution of Delaware from colony to state. *(Courtesy of Delaware Division of Historical and Cultural Affairs)*

ing at Elkton, Maryland, the enemy troops set forth on a path that took them to Cooch's Bridge, where they were met by American troops in a skirmish that was the only Revolutionary War action fought in Delaware. The British and Hessian troops then passed through Newark, Delaware, and headed for the Brandywine River at Chadds Ford, Pennsylvania, where they were met by General George Washington's full army. The invaders won the Battle of the Brandywine and continued their march to capture Philadelphia.

Following their victory, the British briefly occupied Wilmington, but did not march on to seize the defenseless town of New Castle. They did, however, achieve the control of the Delaware River up to and including Philadelphia that their warships had failed to gain the previous year. British seamen visited New Castle to buy food, liquor, and other goods and services with no difficulty. A secretary to General Howe noted that the principal residents of New Castle had fled in anticipation of the enemy's arrival. The town, he sneered, was "small and its buildings mean and scattered." After the British abandoned Philadelphia in 1778, New Castle was no longer subject to enemy visits.

A generation later, during the War of 1812, New Castle girded itself once again, this time for an attack that never came. In 1809 the United States government built an arsenal on New Castle's Green in preparation for the possibility of war. In 1813 British ships entered the Delaware Bay and bombarded Lewes, but they did not sail up the river. Shortly after the war ended, the United States government undertook to build a series of protective coastal forts to prevent future foreign attack. The site chosen for the Delaware River fort was a small island called Pea Patch, located several miles south of New Castle. The construction of Fort Delaware there made the battery at New Castle redundant. Although Fort Delaware's guns have never been tested by enemy invaders, during the Civil War the fort served as a prisoner of war camp.

In 1797 the Delaware General Assembly granted New Castle a town government. The legislature appointed a commission consisting of five of the town's leading men to establish New Castle's boundaries, lay out its streets, and begin other urban processes. The law also permitted New Castle's voters to elect a town council, which would assume responsibilities begun by the commission and have the power to raise funds through taxes. Subsequently, New Castle began the long process of paving its streets and sidewalks, providing gutters, and building wharves into deep water.

From the perspective of future historians, the town government's most significant step was its decision to engage Benjamin Henry Latrobe, a nationally recognized architect, engineer, and surveyor, who was then surveying a possible route for a cross-Delmarva canal, to make a complete survey of the town to include its buildings and street elevations. Latrobe carried out his survey in 1804 and 1805. That document provides the most accurate account of how New Castle looked at that time, and was the template for grading the town's streets. In subsequent years hills were leveled and the dirt deposited in marshland to provide new spaces for buildings and better health for residents.

The first decade of the nineteenth century was a propitious time for surveying New Castle because the town was enjoying a significant spurt in its development. The unsettled period of the Revolution and immediate post-

The Latrobe Survey included sections of streets to show their current levels and suggestions for re-grading. This section of Third Street, then called Orange Street, faced the Green. The Dutch House, not shown on the section map, stood at the far right in a low spot. After the street was raised, it became necessary to step down to enter the dwelling. *(Courtesy Delaware Public Archives)*

revolution period had ended as the new Republic began under the United States Constitution. There was a sense of security, of economic growth, and of new possibilities. New Castle's leading men, most of them lawyers, having endured peripatetic lives during the previous three decades, could now settle down in the county seat, where legal business was growing. It was this period that saw the construction of handsome houses in the new Federal style, most built close to the courthouse along the streets that bordered the Green. The owners of those houses typically also owned one or more farms nearby where they also maintained homes for their families' use, especially during the hot summer months.

Joseph Scott, a visitor to New Castle in 1807, was impressed by the town's appearance. "New Castle," he wrote "… contains about 160 houses and 1200 inhabitants. A great many of the houses have been built within these few years, and some of them in handsome style." Latrobe, who was living in New Castle while he worked on his surveys, did not entirely share that favorable opinion. He found most of the town's leading men to be narrow, provincial, self-absorbed, and tight-fisted. Anyone of genuine talent in business, he believed, was sure to move on to a more promising place.

Despite his grumbling, the town that Latrobe drew was a significantly more handsome place than it had been thirty years earlier. A number of the

THE SURVEY THAT SHAPED A TOWN

By the end of the eighteenth century, New Castle's town commissioners decided to set the town's boundaries, create a town plan, and establish street and building regulations. When the town's first attempt proved inadequate, the commissioners turned for help to the best known architect and engineer working in the mid-Atlantic area: Benjamin Henry Latrobe. Latrobe agreed to survey the town and produce a map within a year that would include street gradients to be used in planning for future road improvements and town development. The entrepreneurial Latrobe used two of his students, Robert Mills and William Strickland, to meet his deadline.

The town commissioners responsible for the project chafed at Latrobe's seemingly slow pace and threatened to void his contract. But the finished product must have far surpassed whatever expectations they might have had. Latrobe presented them with a book that contained fourteen pages of drawings, beginning with a full map of the town. In addition to the survey data, the plan included the location, shape, and material of construction of every building in town, with the names of owners or renters attached. The work also included sections of the developed streets from The Strand to Fourth, Chestnut to South, with current gradients and recommendations for re-grading.

Along some of the book's pages of street sections were depictions of building facades carefully rendered and beautifully water colored. It is a *tour de force*. But the book contained still more: a watercolor drawing on the title page and an essay, "References to the Plan and Section of the town of New Castle." Latrobe's goal was to provide the town with a plan that would guide subsequent development. And so it did for most of the nineteenth century.

The Latrobe plan for street re-grading was designed to make the town as flat as possible. The execution of that plan resulted in some striking changes for existing buildings. The relation of two of New Castle's most iconic buildings to the land is illustrative. The re-grading of Third Street upward requires people to step down into the Dutch House, while the removal of the hill on which the courthouse was built has left that building standing on a raised terrace.

Benjamin Henry Latrobe rightfully gets credit for the town survey of New Castle in 1804-05. He oversaw the whole project, did some of the survey work, painted the handsome title illustration, and, most particularly, wrote the accompanying essay. That essay was in essence a full-blown document for urban development. But Latrobe needed the help of his two students, Robert Mills and William Strickland. Mills has not received his due recognition, for he is generally credited with creating the final drawings. Strickland's contribution to the project is uncertain. He spent less time than Mills in New Castle and was by then not on good terms with Latrobe. As a totality, those three men brought a formidable triumvirate of talent to the New Castle project. Imagine this small town on the Delaware River having three of the best architect-engineers of the new nation working on its plan.

Each of these men undertook major architectural and engineering projects throughout the mid-Atlantic and southern states. All three worked on a full range of projects and in multiple styles, but each championed Greek Revival and then Classical Revival styles.

Watercolor by Benjamin Henry Latrobe of the Green from the Courthouse to the Academy. Immanuel Church sits behind the wall to the right of the Academy; Aull's Row is at the far end of the path across the Green; and sails in the harbor suggest a busy port. *(Courtesy of Delaware Public Archives)*

houses in New Castle that are most admired today were constructed by lawyers and political figures during the four decades after the Revolution, the era known in architectural style as the "Federal."

New Castle owed its revival to its continuing importance as a county seat and to its significance in shipping. No enterprise was more important to the newly independent United States than the development of transportation links to connect the disparate parts of a large and expanding nation. In the early days of the Republic, geography and technology worked to New Castle's benefit. At the beginning of the nineteenth century, the town's harbor was the last landing for ships bound across the sea from the busy port of Philadelphia. Ships sailing down the Delaware River from Philadelphia docked at New Castle, the last port they would visit in the United States, to buy fresh provisions, including livestock.

New Castle also offered the best place along the Delaware River to cross the Delmarva Peninsula. Travelers to and from Philadelphia to Baltimore or Washington, D.C., would take a sailing vessel, or later a steamboat, down the Delaware River to New Castle, then cross the peninsula in a stage coach to the hamlet of Frenchtown, Maryland, where they would board another boat for the journey across the Chesapeake Bay to Baltimore. People in transit

BENJAMIN HENRY LATROBE'S VIEWS OF NEW CASTLE

Several years after Benjamin Henry Latrobe produced his plan for the re-grading of New Castle's streets, he revisited the town on a layover in a trip from Philadelphia to Frenchtown, Maryland. Clearly irritated by the fourteen-hour delay in his journey, he vented his spleen in his private journal with a negative assessment of the town:

New Castle is the <u>Gravesend</u> of Philadelphia. Of course the usual conveniences for the accommodation of seafaring men are found in plenty and of the coarsest sort. And as a <u>little</u> country town it has all the petty scandal, curiosity, envy and hatred which distinguishes little towns all over the world.

Latrobe was equally acerbic in his view of the town's leading citizens, particularly those he had interacted with during his time in the village. Latrobe does not provide names for his "character sketches," but based on research, the editors of his papers do. Only Caleb Bennett, the proprietor of an inn at 6 The Strand and later governor of Delaware, fares well. He befriended Latrobe's wife during an emergency when Latrobe was travelling. Latrobe's negative assessment of Kensey Johns is in no small measure based on their engagement in a joint land speculation deal while both were involved in the Chesapeake and Delaware Canal Corporation.

Caleb Bennett. *He is a good man, a great politician, a flaming democrat, and an adorer of Bounaparte … . He is loved and laughed at by every body, and though he keeps a very bad tavern, he makes money on it … . He is the only man, who, … ever did us a kind office.*

George Read, Jr. *…a small man, but exceedingly pompous. He has built an enormous house, in bad taste, and I think in a very bad situation.*

Kensey Johns. *A man of <u>keen</u> intelligence, a political Camel eon [sic], in pecuniary honesty a bankrupt, but very rich, and from nothing possessed like all other Lawyers of immense tracts of Land in the state.*

James Booth. *Judge Booth is, excepting always my friend Bennet [sic], the best and more accomplished man in the place, but not openhearted … .*

There are half a dozen good natured men besides in this place. … None of them were ever suspected of giving away anything in charity, or acquiring any thing by their <u>genius</u>.

But to do no wrong in Newcastle is praise worthy.

It is no wonder indeed that talent and worth should be rare here. Newcastle cannot be a commercial town while Philadelphia exists. As soon as a merchant acquires capital, the field of Newcastle is too small for him and he moves away. Two exceptions exist however in the houses, of Riddle and Bird, and of [Thomas] Bond, who are supposed to have grown rich by supplying ships with Stock for their Voyages, a business in which they continue and on a large scale.

—The Journals of Benjamin Henry Latrobe, 1799-1820 . . ., pp. 35-42.

typically stayed overnight in a New Castle inn and ate and drank in one of its taverns. Many famous people of the day passed through New Castle, including the Marquis de Lafayette on his grand tour of the United States in 1824,

THE ICE PIERS

Seven ice piers stand in the Delaware River near the New Castle shore between Harmony Street and Battery Park. They were built between 1803 and 1882 by the United States government. The earliest of these piers was the first federally-financed transportation improvement project undertaken in Delaware. There had been earlier piers built in the 1790s with funds from a state-sponsored lottery, but those had proved to be inadequate. The granite blocks that can be seen above water are really shells filled with rubble. They rest on submerged wooden cribs.

The purpose of the piers was to protect wooden-hulled ships from ice floes, especially during violent winter storms. By the end of the nineteenth century the introduction of ships built with iron or steel hulls diminished the importance of the piers to the safety of river commerce. In the summer months the piers have remained attractive as diving platforms for some of New Castle's youngsters.

President Andrew Jackson, and his fellow westerners Davy Crockett and the Indian chief Black Hawk.

But new innovations in transportation being introduced in America changed patterns of travel and commerce in ways that limited New Castle's commercial development. The first assault on New Castle's significance was the Chesapeake and Delaware Canal. Built in the 1820s, the canal was dug several miles below New Castle at a location that took advantage of existing waterways and a relatively level crossing of the peninsula. A new town called Delaware City marked the canal's entrance to the Delaware River. The canal offered an all-water shipping route to link Philadelphia and Wilmington to Baltimore without engaging New Castle at all.

In an effort to protect as much of its role in interstate transportation as possible, New Castle's leaders turned to a yet newer technology: the steam railway. In 1832 a group comprised of local and Philadelphia entrepreneurs completed the New Castle and Frenchtown Railroad, which stretched twenty-seven miles across the peninsula, and replaced the stage-coach route as a passenger line. It was Delaware's first railroad and was among the pioneering rail lines in the United States. But the primacy of the New Castle and Frenchtown Railroad was short-lived. Less than six years later a longer and better-financed railroad called the Philadelphia, Wilmington and Baltimore, or PW&B, began operation. Whereas the New Castle and Frenchtown offered a shortened passage between two lengthy water journeys on the Delaware River and Chesapeake Bay, passengers on the PW&B could travel by rail from Philadelphia to Baltimore with only a brief passage by ferry across the Susquehanna River at Perryville, Maryland. As its name suggests, the PW&B stopped in Wilmington, bypassing New Castle altogether.

Constrained by the Chesapeake and Delaware Canal about seven miles to the south and the PW&B Railroad to the north, New Castle lost much of its role in trans-peninsular travel. Nonetheless, throughout the age of steam, river steamboats bearing passengers and cargo continued to stop at New Castle en route up the river to Wilmington

Advertisement with fares and schedule for the NC &FT Railroad. Its earliest passenger cars looked like stagecoaches. *(Courtesy of Delaware Historical Society)*

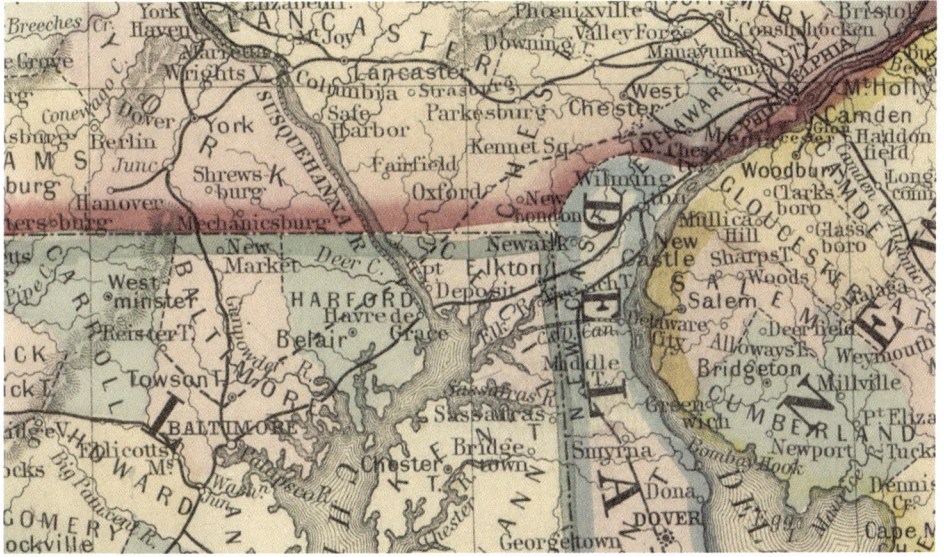

Detail of a four-state map of 1860 showing railroad and canal routes through northern Delaware. *(Courtesy of University of Delaware Library, Newark, Del.)*

Late-nineteenth-century oil painting by Frank F. English of the side-wheel steamer *Thomas Clyde* plying the waters of the Delaware River. *(Courtesy of Hagley Museum and Library)*

and Philadelphia, across to New Jersey, and down the river to beach resorts along the bay. Late-nineteenth-century residents of New Castle could board steamboats such as the *Major Reybold* or the *Thomas Clyde* or travel by train the thirty-five miles to Philadelphia, which they called "the city," to shop, see a play, or hear a concert.

New Castle was Philadelphia's junior partner. Out-bound ships from the big city's busy harbor continued to stop at New Castle to take on the freshest possible food provisions, including animals, before venturing down the river to the Atlantic. New Castle also served as a harbor of refuge for ships bound for the ports of Wilmington and Philadelphia when winter ice closed their harbors. The pull of the tides was strong at New Castle so that the granite ice-breaking piers that still stand in New Castle's harbor could break the ice near the river's channel. But even in New Castle, the river bank area froze small boats in place.

Building the Community

During the first three decades of the nineteenth century the citizens of New Castle did their best to make their town commercially competitive.

The community worked for and hoped for a more promising outcome to their commercial ambitions, and in many ways the town continued to make progress. Aided by funds from the Trustees of the Common, the town built an Academy on the Green in 1801, a private school designed to educate those local students whose parents could afford the modest tuition. Other community improvements from that era included the creation of a subscription library and the establishment of a voluntary fire company. In 1823 the town erected a town hall, which also provided space for meetings and for fire equipment.

The new building was hardly completed when, on April 26, 1824, fire broke out in an outbuilding or warehouse at the south end of The Strand, then called Water Street. Winds spread the flames to a nearby lumberyard and then carried the blaze up both sides of the street. Everybody in town joined in efforts to fight the fire and to save furniture and other valuables from the buildings that were threatened. A Wilmington newspaper recorded the chaotic, sad scene: "Never have we seen a spectacle more distressing than this once beautiful town now presents. From the north to the south end of Water Street little is to be seen but tottering walls and solitary chimneys."

Detail from *Map of New Castle County* (Philadelphia: Rea and Price, 1849), showing Town Hall with wooden market stalls behind. This is the only known image of New Castle done by A. V. Lesley, noted doctor, civic leader, and artist. *(Courtesy of New Castle Historical Society)*

Remarkably, no one died, but twenty-three families lost their homes and nearly as many businesses were destroyed. Among the charred remains was the home of the late George Read, the lawyer and politician who had helped lead Delaware through the Revolution. The garden of his son George Read II's grand house now occupies the site of the statesman's home. Thus, the

FIGHTING THE FIRE OF 1824

The conflagration of 1824 destroyed a large number of buildings along both sides of The Strand, and frightened those who lived on the street and in the town. What is sometimes forgotten is the enormous human effort that went into fighting the fire and saving belongings. Maria Booth Rogers experienced the fire first-hand, and her account to her husband, away on business, written in the heat of the fire, captures the fear as well as the spontaneous outpouring of assistance of those living in town and beyond in New Castle's hour of need.

In 1824 Maria Rogers, daughter of Chief Justice James Booth, Sr., and wife of Delaware Attorney General James Rogers, was approaching 40 and lived at 214 Delaware Street. She had been born, lived, and eventually died in New Castle. This was her town and her neighbors. She, like others, did all she could to help. By the time she wrote the first part of her letter, it was 2 a.m. on April 27, nearly 11 hours after the fire had broken out, and she was exhausted, but the danger that the flames could still ignite the marsh grass along the river bank remained and kept people on the alert. Later that day after hard rains brought the fire under control, she wrote the conclusion of her letter.

You can have no idea of the scene of horror it exhibited. Imagine the whole on fire ... all the back buildings on both sides of Water Street [now The Strand], the females crying, and yet very actively engaged in carrying water. I am almost exhausted with fatigue. I have been carrying water, and furniture, all the afternoon—the furniture is lying about in the streets, the market house filled, the arsenal, and almost all the street the market house stands in, some in the meeting house, and in the church yard. ...

It was really distressing this morning to walk round the town and see the desolation it has made, and those that have not where to lay their heads, except taken in by their neighbors, looking for their furniture, some in one place and some in another. However it is impossible to give you a description of the scene of distress, and yet we have reason to be thankful, that no lives were lost. ...

—Boothhurst Collection, Delaware Historical Society

flames destroyed the home of New Castle's most famous citizen, but spared the town's most distinguished house located only a few feet away.

In the wake of the tragedy the town demonstrated a "can do" spirit. Town fathers wrote to America's major cities to ask for help. Addressing the lead-

Houses on land side of The Strand, as shown on the Latrobe Survey, that were lost in the fire of 1824. *(Courtesy of the Delaware Public Archives)*

ers of Boston, the New Castle men recalled how their town had contributed to aid Boston in Revolutionary days. Their request earned a generous gift

of $900. Other cities were similarly helpful, and builders speedily reconstructed the lost homes and businesses. The Strand that one sees today is testimony to those efforts.

The New Castle County Courthouse, which fortunately stood more than a block away from the blaze, was the town's largest and most prominent building. By the mid-nineteenth century it had become part of a complex of related structures that included the sheriff's

Detail from the Latrobe Survey of the George Read House, now the side garden of the George Read II House. *(Courtesy of Delaware Public Archives)*

Detail of the A.V. Lesley engraving from the Rea and Price map of 1849 showing the courthouse and attached poorhouse and jail, subsequently replaced by a prison and Sheriff's House. *(Courtesy of New Castle Historical Society)*

house and the county jail. The most prominent feature in the jail yard was a scaffold that included a pillory and whipping post. A stone wall separated this grim place from nearby market stalls, a school, and two churches. The pillory and whipping post were visible from the street and market place, where crowds gathered to witness the sheriff laying the lashes onto the backs of manacled prisoners. Hangings drew even larger crowds of gawkers.

In the courthouse, lawyers and judges met to try cases not only for the county and state courts, but also for the United States District Court for Delaware. In 1848, Roger B. Taney, the Chief Justice of the United States, presided over the most famous trial ever held in the building. Thomas Garrett, a Quaker merchant of Wilmington, and John Hunn of Middletown were accused of helping a family of run-away slaves escape to the free state of Pennsylvania. The jury found in favor of the aggrieved slave owners and the defendants were fined a massive sum. Thomas Garrett lost all his money, but not his resolve to assist slaves seeking freedom. Harriet Beecher Stowe heard about the case and included it in fictionalized form in her highly influential anti-slavery novel, *Uncle Tom's Cabin*.

Delaware remained a slave state until the Thirteenth Amendment to the United States Constitution was enacted after the Civil War. In spite of their state's reluctance to eradicate slavery, most Delawareans, especially those of New Castle County, had abandoned the institution before the war occurred. The federal census of 1850 reported that the town of New Castle had no remaining slaves. In that year there were about 250 black residents in the town, accounting for roughly one in five residents of New Castle. Most African-American men were laborers, although some had listed occupations in transportation and the building trades. Several

Restored courtroom on the first floor of New Castle's county courthouse from 1752 to 1881. *(Courtesy of Delaware Division of Historical and Cultural Affairs)*

owned businesses, including a hotel and an oyster restaurant. Black women typically worked as house servants. A significant number of the town's black residents, both single people and families, lived in the white households where they worked. Others lived in homes scattered among lower-class white households at the edges of the town. Two black Methodist churches served the community by the time of the Civil War.

New Castle's white population exhibited mixed feelings about the Civil War. New Castle was a border town in a border state. In the election of 1860 with four men on the ballot for president, the southern Democrat, John C. Breckenridge, won the majority of votes cast in New Castle, and the Republican, Abraham Lincoln, won the least. At a meeting in the courthouse, abolitionists were denounced and states rights proclaimed. Enthusiasm for the Union cause was dim. Some young men volunteered to join the United States Army, while others formed a Home Guard company whose allegiance, other than safe-guarding the town, was unclear. During the war, some residents held bazaars and picnics to raise money and provide food and clothing to aid Confederate prisoners housed at Fort Delaware. On one memorable occasion in July 1864, government authorities disrupted such a Confederate prisoners' aid picnic at McCrone's Woods near Hare's Corner. About twenty-five New Castle area men were arrested and imprisoned at Fort McHenry in Baltimore for a week before being released.

The Industrial Age

The introduction of steam engines made large-scale manufacturing possible in New Castle. Steam-powered factories began to appear in the town in the 1830s. The factories increased in size and number for the next hundred years or more, encouraged by town leaders and by the expansion of railroad lines that connected the town to regional and national networks. Those advantages attracted industrial entrepreneurs, especially from Philadelphia, and changed New Castle from a commercial town to one of industry.

In 1833, a group of New Castle's own businessmen, including transportation entrepreneur Thomas Janvier, banker James Couper, and nearby estate owner Charles I. du Pont, created a foundry called the New Castle Manufacturing Company to build locomotives for the newly opened New Castle and Frenchtown Railroad and for other railroads in the region. The factory was located in the west part of town, immediately beside the New Castle and Frenchtown Railroad tracks at today's West Fifth and South streets. The company barely survived the economic downturn after the Panic of 1837 but was able to produce eleven locomotives by 1840 and to continue production until the late 1850s, when it was sold to another steam-engine producer.

JULIA JEFFERSON, THE CONFEDERATE PRISONERS' ANGEL OF MERCY

Julia Ann Jefferson (1841-1918) came from a family of strong Democrats and was openly sympathetic to the Southern Cause. Her uncle, Samuel Jefferson, was an elector for Breckenridge, the pro-Southern Democratic candidate for President of the United States in 1860, and was himself an unsuccessful gubernatorial candidate in Delaware in 1862. Her father, Elihu R. Jefferson, owned 5 The Strand near the harbor on the northeast corner of Delaware Street and The Strand. He was one of New Castle's leading citizens, a prosperous merchant, the presiding officer of the Trustees of the Common, and a long-time member of the Board of Trustees of the New Castle branch of the Farmers Bank.

When the Union turned Fort Delaware into a prison for captured Confederate soldiers, Julia organized and led a very successful effort in New Castle to assist those poorly-cared-for men. Under her direction both men and women of the town made contributions of food, tobacco, clothing, bedding, and money to provide for the prisoners. They also held picnics and other fund-raising events to assist the cause. It was at such an event on July 28, 1864, that a group of men, including Julia's brother, were arrested and briefly held in prison. Julia herself, although not imprisoned, was required to take an oath of allegiance to the United States.

Julia Jefferson became a frequent visitor to the nearby island fortress. She always came bearing a smile as well as food, blankets, and even occasional luxuries such as cigars. Her activities had the full support of the prison commandant, who gave her permission to come "at pleasure." The United States government was so overstretched that its officers welcomed assistance to keep the prisoners as healthy and content as possible. She particularly befriended the fort's surgeon, who applauded her humanitarian efforts.

To the prisoners she was truly "an angel of mercy" as many of their letters of thankful gratitude attest. "We are cut off from all communication with our friends at present," as one prisoner said. The men incarcerated at the fort had little to look forward to except for "the bright smile of several from New Castle, whose deeds of kindness can never be forgotten." A decade after the war ended, Julia married James Stedman Dungan, a New Castle merchant.

—Papers of Julia Jefferson, Delaware Historical Society

One casualty of the Panic of 1837 was the railroad itself. The New Castle and Frenchtown Railroad sold out to the Philadelphia, Wilmington and Baltimore Railroad in 1839, but the connection of the two railroads did not take place for over a decade. By the time of the Civil War, the line from Wilmington, initially called the New Castle and Wilmington Railroad, had been completed, connecting with the slightly reconfigured NC&FT tracks. The old NC&FT then was renamed the Delaware Road. Over time all of those tracks and additional spurs to factories passed through changes of ownership and names, with each change expanding the town's reach into regional and national markets.

The expansion of the railroad on the west side of town from the river inland along South and Young streets encouraged ever-more industries to locate there, particularly because New Castle did not object to the construction of additional spur lines to serve new sites. By the end of the nineteenth century, seven sets of tracks ran into the area now redeveloped as Battery Park. New industries included a large steam-driven flour mill, several textile mills, and iron and steel manufactories.

In 1857 James G. Shaw of Chester, Pennsylvania, came to New Castle to be a real-estate developer. He purchased nearly 200 acres of farmland just outside the western edge of the town from Kensey Johns, Jr., and planned to develop it as an industrial-residential addition to New Castle. His vision became a reality for the land he purchased became

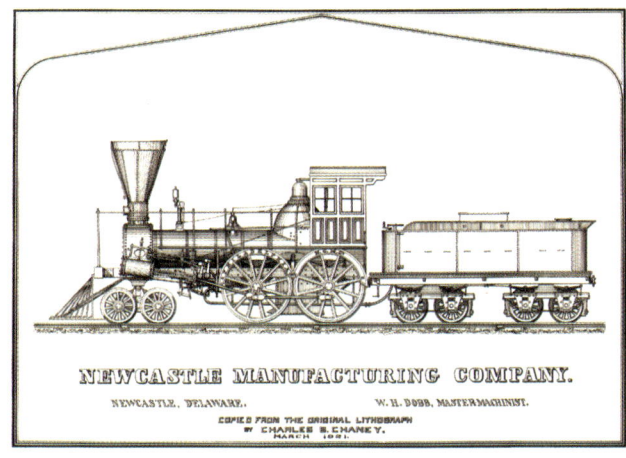

NEWCASTLE MANUFACTURING COMPANY.

NEWCASTLE, DELAWARE.   W. H. DOBB, MASTER MACHINIST.

COPIED FROM THE ORIGINAL LITHOGRAPH
BY CHARLES B. CHANEY.
MARCH 1881.

The New Castle Manufacturing Company produced this engine, named "Philadelphia," in 1852. *(Courtesy of Delaware Historical Society)*

Shawtown. In 1860 Shaw established the Triton Spinning Mill at Ninth and Washington streets. The mill employed well over one hundred people, many

Layout of New Castle in 1868 shows railroad lines and factories dominating the west side of town. From *Atlas of the State of Delaware* (Philadelphia: Pomeroy and Beers, 1868). *(Courtesy of New Castle Historical Society)*

of whom lived in Shawtown. When Shaw's cotton mill closed a generation later, its buildings were taken over by the Deemer Steel Company.

Another textile mill was constructed nearby in the early 1870s by James G. Knowles, Shaw's former business partner, to make woolen yarn for use in men's wear. That mill burned and was rebuilt twice before it closed in 1900. The Wilmington Fibre Specialty Company later took over that property as well as that of a flour mill also located near the railroad and close to the road to Delaware City.

New Castle's most prominent entrepreneur during the Civil War years was Pennsylvanian Thomas T. Tasker of Philadelphia. Tasker's life story presents yet another illustration of the American Dream in action. He was born in Yorkshire, England, in 1799 and learned the machinist trade there before coming to Philadelphia in 1819. The invention of gas illumination created a need for pipelines to carry the gas. Tasker and his business partner, Henry

G. Morris, began manufacturing gas pipes and went on to build the Philadelphia Gas Works.

In 1857 Tasker expanded his business beyond Philadelphia when he created the New Castle Gas Company to supply the new form of illumination to homeowners and the town's street lamps. But Tasker did not limit his business activities to supplying gas. In 1865 he opened a large steam flour mill in New Castle that took advantage of the town's access to both river harbor and railroad connections. Located on Fifth Street at an intersection

James G. Shaw, mill owner and developer. *(Courtesy of New Castle Historical Society)*

Thomas T. Tasker, leading industrialist of nineteenth-century New Castle. *(Courtesy of New Castle Historical Society)*

with the New Castle and Frenchtown Railroad track, the mill required the construction of multiple railroad sidings that ran to a pier in the present-day Battery Park.

Tasker was an inveterate entrepreneur. He bought much of Shawtown from its namesake and also constructed New Castle's first waterworks. Water was pumped from the Nonesuch Creek, a tributary of the Christina River, to a basin on the northwest edge of the town that gave its name to present-day Basin Road.

In 1872 Thomas Tasker sold his flour mill to the firm of Thomas Lea

Tasker Iron Works was located on the west side of New Castle at the water's edge between Johnson and Clymer streets. This image of 1876 shows river traffic as well as over a dozen smokestacks. *(Courtesy of New Castle Historical Society)*

& Sons of Wilmington and shifted his focus to iron manufacturing. He was already a partner in the Pascal Iron Works in Philadelphia, which made iron castings. His new business in New Castle was similar. Called the Delaware Iron Company, the business occupied a large site served by a railroad spur that sprawled over thirty-five acres at the river's edge south of town between Clymer and Johnson streets. The works were capable of making one hundred tons of iron pipes daily to be used in gas and water mains. The Tasker works and the other factories required additional railroad spurs that crisscrossed New Castle's streets and dominated the southwest area of the town.

Although Thomas Tasker continued to live in Philadelphia, his married daughter moved to New Castle, as did his son, Stephen, who managed the company's affairs in the town. Thomas Tasker himself was a significant presence in the town, not just for his employment of many residents, but also for his support of the Methodist churches there. Tasker was a lifelong, strong Methodist who sometimes appeared in New Castle to preach at the Methodist Church on Delaware Street. After his retirement from business he dedicated his later years to religious work and to charity before his death in Philadelphia in 1892.

Selden Scranton Deemer, a native of Reading, Pennsylvania, learned steel-making from his father in Philadelphia. He came to New Castle in 1904 as

OCTOBER 23, 1878:
A DEVASTATING DAY OF FIRE AND RAIN

An autumn hurricane in 1878 roared out of the Caribbean Sea and up the east coast of the United States on a track that ran west of Delaware, putting the state on the storm's most dangerous side. The worst of the storm hit in the morning hours of October 23, leaving behind a trail of devastation along the Delaware River. The storm did not dump record amounts of rain nor did the winds match records for highest speed or longest duration. Yet, for one brief period the hurricane produced a confluence of weather elements that spelled maximum disaster.

Modest levels of rain accompanied by very high winds began during the night of October 22. Then about 7:30 the next morning those strong winds ripped the roof off the boiler room of the New Castle Woolen Mills at Seventh and Washington streets, sending flames from the boilers into stored wool. Those flames shot everywhere, and the fire roared out of control, forcing female workers to jump from second-floor windows. By the time the fire companies could respond, the mills were lost. But the fire companies still had their hands full battling the blaze that shifting winds had sent toward the Lea flour mills northwest of the cotton mills.

As the winds roared and the flames soared, water rose at an alarming rate in the Delaware River and surrounding creeks. Tidal surges broke through the banks of the Delaware River north and south of New Castle, inundating the marshes and for a time isolating the town. Those surges washed out the bulkhead at Thomas Tasker's Delaware Iron Works south of town, flooded the gas works, and drove a schooner from the river a mile into the marshes. To the north a woman was swept off a boat. Wind and water lifted a house off its foundation and carried it two miles into the marshes. Amazingly, as it floated away, people saw two men cheerfully waving goodbye from second-floor windows. In town, water rose to a height of four feet above the river's banks, sweeping cargo from docks, while high winds slammed ships, sinking several at the Delaware Street wharf and at the Battery. Roofs and even buildings throughout the town also succumbed to the wind.

All townspeople could do was wait out the worst of the storm and then begin to assess the damage and plan for salvage and rebuilding. When it was over, the newspaper reported that the most unfortunate victim of the storm was not the owner of the cotton mill, but Israel Riddings, a carpenter and ship owner. Captain Riddings not only lost his ship and its cargo, he also lost all of his carpenter and shipwright tools when the building where they were stored collapsed—and all of his children were thrown out of work when the cotton mill burned down.

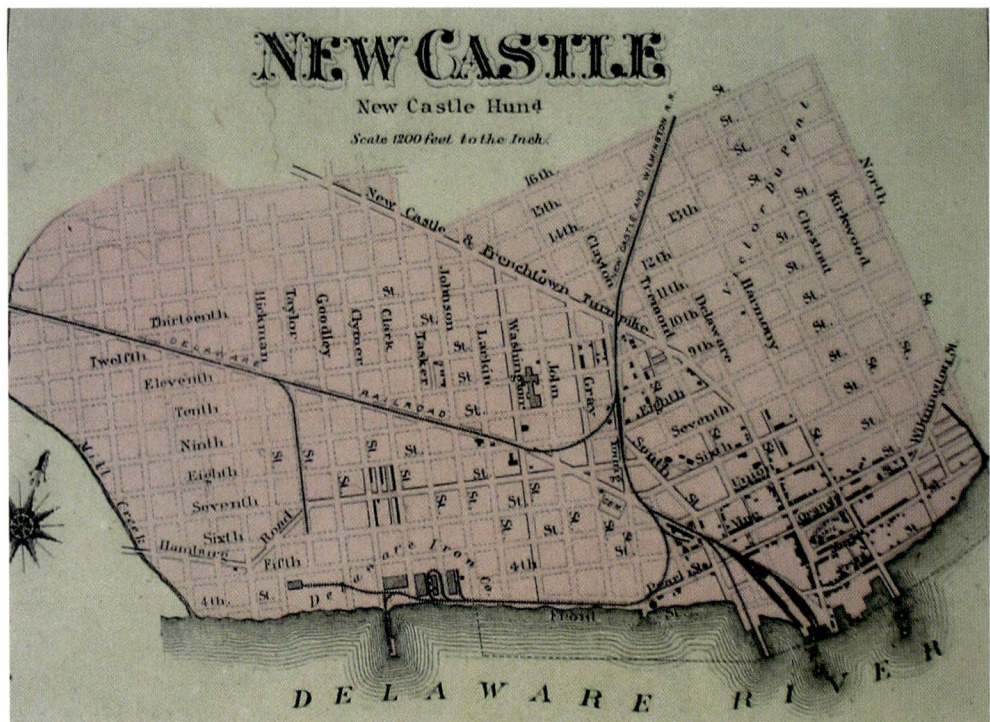

New Castle in 1881. From *Map of New Castle County* (Philadelphia: G.M. Hopkins, 1881). *(Courtesy of New Castle Historical Society)*

superintendent of the Brylgon Steel Company, a casting mill located just north of the town's center. Five years later he began construction of his own steel-casting company on the land formerly occupied by Shaw's factory. Deemer's Steel operated there well into the twentieth century. In 1923, after selling that company, Selden Deemer created an amusement park south of New Castle on the Delaware River that was designed to attract the recreational river-steamer trade. His factory buildings have since been replaced by a large garden-style apartment complex.

Industrialization reversed the precipitous drop of over fifty percent in the town's population that had begun in the decade from 1840 to 1850. At their height in the late nineteenth century, New Castle's factories employed hundreds of people, including local people, both black and white, as well as many immigrants from Ireland, Italy, Germany, and Poland. The inflow of new residents led to the construction of clusters of small houses along streets throughout the town. Richard J. Dobbins, a major building contractor in Philadelphia, built rows of workers' housing near to the factories southwest of town in the 1870s to a commodate workers at the iron manufactory. Dobbinsville remains as testimony to that enterprising builder and to the workers of that era.

Most of the immigrants to New Castle were Roman Catholics. An earlier generation of Catholics had built a small church in the town, but it was only when their numbers

Further south on the Delaware River from New Castle's west-side factories lay Deemer's Beach with its amusement park. *(Courtesy of Hagley Museum and Library)*

swelled that in 1870 they were able to build Saint Peter the Apostle Church and later add a handsome bell tower and a parochial school at Fifth and Harmony streets.

In an era that experienced such rapid economic development, it proved difficult to keep any of those industrial businesses for long. Most went out of business within a few decades of their construction. In 1900 the Lea Flour Mill closed, as did a woolen mill that had employed two hundred hands. Tasker's iron company closed its doors soon after. Why? People at the time blamed the "Trusts," huge consolidated corporations such as General Mills and Carnegie Steel that had all the advantages of locations, capitalization, and new technologies.

In New Castle the factories that closed were mostly located on the town's southwest side. The factories and the jobs that they had provided were sorely missed. The Trustees of the Common and other town leaders sought to attract new enterprises by offering enticements. A brochure published in 1915 proclaimed New Castle's offer of a ten-year tax exemption for new business. But that was not all. The town could also provide "free sites for any line of manufacture and also cheap land along the river suitable for blast furnaces,

Penn-Seaboard Steel Company north of New Castle's historic center, ca. 1925. *(Courtesy of Hagley Museum and Library)*

with plenty of low land for dumping slag, etc."

Such inducements, plus cash, led to a third wave of industrialization. Two steel-casting mills, Baldt and Brylgon (with Selden Deemer as superintendent), located northeast of town, adjacent to Immanuel Episcopal Church's Glebe Farm. These companies were later subsumed into one gigantic whole as the Penn-Seaboard Steel Company. Their smoke stacks rose, clearly visible from the river, to proclaim proudly New Castle's industrial enterprise. About a mile south of town, the Bethlehem Steel Company built a large munitions plant during World War I.

By 1900 heavy industries lined the borders of the Delaware River and its major tributaries from Trenton, New Jersey, to Delaware City. Those

World War I parade float in front of Bethlehem Steel Loading Company, ca. 1918, touts the company's safety record. *(Courtesy of Hagley Museum and Library)*

factories doomed a once-important source of food and income for New Castle: fish. Both shad and sturgeon are ocean-dwelling fish that return every spring to their freshwater spawning grounds. The vast numbers of shad and sturgeon that annually swam up the Delaware River had been crucial

THE BIG BLAST AT NEW CASTLE

During World War I, the Bethlehem Steel Company built a large munitions plant along the Delaware River about a mile south of New Castle. Here a workforce of men and women packed TNT and shrapnel into shell casings to be used by the Allied armies. Danger lurked everywhere in the munitions plant, and all who worked at the plant had to have a tattoo for identification purposes in case of a disaster. Even without an explosion, the work of a powder monkey, as a shell packer was called, was unpleasant, for the piric acid used in making the powder often turned flesh dark yellow. The plant's most famous employee was Florence Bayard Hilles, a member of Delaware's most prominent political family and the state's leading suffragist, who volunteered for war work to demonstrate her patriotism.

On the morning of December 13, 1917, explosions rocked the plant, dropped shells on the southern edge of New Castle, and suspended or disrupted train and ship traffic. Fire quickly swept through a frame building filled with thousands of shells loaded with TNT but fortunately not yet loaded with shrapnel. As the fire hit the loaded shells, they exploded. The bombardment of about 4,000 shells lasted more than an hour and resonated far beyond New Castle. A rumor quickly spread through the town that river artillery defenses were firing at enemy ships.

After the fire burned out and the air cleared, only one employee was found to have lost his life. If the day shift of 500 workers had been on site rather than sitting on street cars stalled by a breakdown at the power plant, the toll might well have been far higher.

to the diets of the native peoples and to the European colonists who followed. In the nineteenth century as many as one hundred or more New

Castle residents were commercial fishermen. The fishermen in their small boats could be seen every spring laying their nets. Millions of pounds of shad were caught in huge nets as large as a mile long that were attached to floating buoys. Shad fishermen found the bigger, bony-skinned sturgeon a hindrance until the price of caviar rose in the 1890s. Then the Dela-

Fishermen stand at the end of Jefferson's Wharf in front of a fish warehouse and above a portion of the town's fishing fleet. *(Courtesy of New Castle Historical Society)*

SHAD CAPITAL OF DELAWARE

I like him baked, I like him broiled,
Or even fried,—but never nail
His silver beauty to a plank,
Leave on both head and tail,
And baste him with a slice of pork
(The fattest to be had,)
And roast him at a roaring fire,
Behold, the perfect shad!

This ode by an unknown poet pays homage to the most important fish in New Castle's history. Since time immemorial everyone has loved the shad and its roe, and none seemed better than those caught in the Delaware River around New Castle. First sold dockside, the reach of the town's shad expanded with the advent of water-tank railroad cars. At the height of the business at the turn of the twentieth century as many as 30,000 shad could be shipped out of New Castle in a single day, earning the town the nickname "Fishtown."

Fishing was an art and a science, but mostly it was very hard work with long hours in all kinds of weather during the spring fishing season. Some claimed that a true fisherman could stand on the dock in early spring and smell the fish approaching. Then off to work the boats would go. Louis E. Eliason, a merchant by profession and a fisherman at heart, described his first-hand observations in an unpublished, undated memoir written at the height of the industry, probably in the 1890s.

… the fishermen would rise at five o'clock in the morning, five days a week and go out into their skiffs with their nets. On the weekends when they were not permitted to fish, they would spend long hours repairing their damaged nets. It was a sight to see the long nets stretched out to dry. These nets were knitted to order and were possibly three quarters of a mile long. The fishermen fitted to them their floats on one side and lead sinkers on the other side so that as the nets were laid off the stern of a slowly moving boat, it would float in a vertical position. When a tide had been fished, the net would be gathered into the hand of a fisherman. And as a second man backed the boat with oars, the first fisherman would draw the net, like a wet rope into the skiff and as he did so each shad tangled in the net would be freed and dropped into compartments made for that purpose. Three hundred to four hundred shad per boat was not unusual for a four or five hour drift. At one time thirty to forty boats operated out of New Castle.

—Nicholas McIntire, *The Best of "Behind the Times …"*
—Daniel P. Johnson, "The J.T. and L.E. Eliason Company …."

ware River fishermen sought the formerly scorned fish, even exporting their eggs to Russia.

Shad skiff "Neptune." (*Courtesy of New Castle Historical Society*)

Skiff with large sturgeon aboard. (*Courtesy of New Castle Historical Society*)

At the beginning of the twentieth century, three fish houses and a large two-story fish shed stood on the wharf at Delaware Street. After 1900, however, the fishing business began to decline due to a combination of overfishing and industrial pollution. By 1940 commercial fishing for shad at New Castle was dead.

While fishing and a few other industries were in eclipse, New Castle soared in the most modern of early-twentieth-century transportation technologies: aviation. In 1927, the year of Charles Lindbergh's solo flight from Long Island to Paris, an Italian aircraft manufacturer named Giuseppe Bellanca, backed by the

Shad nets drying in what is now Battery Park, about 1905. (*Courtesy of New Castle Historical Society*)

View from river looking at coal dock and Jefferson's Wharf with its then many offices and warehouses. (*Courtesy of Delaware Historical Society*)

Bellanca airplane flying above factory and hanger, ca. 1928. *(Courtesy of Delaware Historical Society)*

local flying enthusiast H.B. du Pont, moved his factory from New York to the outskirts of New Castle along the New Castle and Frenchtown Road, now Route 273. Bellanca employed many New Castle residents in his factory, especially Italian-Americans. They produced lightweight aircraft that set numerous records for flying ever-longer distances during the 1920s and the 1930s. Shortly after Lindburgh's historic flight, a Bellanca-built plane flew even further, going from the United States to Germany.

During World War II, the company suspended aircraft design and production to undertake defense work, often done by a large force of women hired from the community. When the Bellanca Aircraft Corporation closed in 1954, other industries took over much of the former airfield, but the company's air-service hangar still stands as a reminder of its historic legacy.

The Age of Industry had renewed New Castle's prosperity and expanded its population. In 1875 the Delaware General Assembly gave New Castle the status of a city with its own mayor and council to oversee the community's expanded responsibilities of government. Other signs of the civic optimism of that time can be seen in the construction of impressive Victorian structures,

Workers at Bellanca during World War II. *(Courtesy of Delaware Public Archives)*

especially the cupola-topped Masonic Hall-Opera House built in 1879-80 on Delaware Street and the hexagon-shaped library built in 1892 on Third Street.

Industry changed the town's landscape and expanded its population at a time when New Castle was forced to relinquish its original function as a government center. In 1879, after decades of struggle in the Delaware General Assembly, New Castle lost the county courts to its rival, Wilmington. New Castle's most historic claim to significance was gone. In 1881 a large, impressive new courthouse was completed in Wilmington on the property that is now Rodney Square. Its architect was Theophilus P. Chandler, who was simultaneously designing New Castle's Opera House. In 1883 the General Assembly gave the old courthouse, formerly the property of New Castle County, to the town. The jail and whipping post, however, continued to serve their function in New Castle until 1901, when the New Castle County Workhouse was constructed at Greenbank near Price's Corner.

Transportation, Revival, and Tourism

Wilmington had won the county seat. It was time for the county's only city and its largest town to find common ground and make up. In 1897 an electric trolley line was constructed from Wilmington to New Castle. The trolleys brought both a new form of transportation and the means to use electricity to light New Castle's street lamps. It was now easy to live in New Castle and work or shop in Wilmington.

In many places, including Wilmington, trolley cars led the way to urban residential expansion, especially to the creation of new boulevards that showcased expensive

Trolley stopped in front of 212 Delaware Street, about 1920. The cupola on the Opera House has since been removed. *(Courtesy of Delaware Historical Society)*

homes. That did not happen in New Castle, where the established families chose to remain in their homes close to the Green with its courthouse, schools, and churches. Trolley car service did, however, encourage the more expansive streetscape of New Castle's developing west side. The industrialization and railroad noise and soot that drove wealthy people in other communities to move further out of town were not a problem in New Castle because the factories and the rail lines that supported them were the ones making the move ever farther from the town's historic center. Topography also played a role in the retention of the town's old residential core. The undeveloped areas closest to New Castle were low-lying, some were even marshy. The best housing sites were already taken.

The two greatest forces that shaped the history of New Castle in the twentieth century were the interwoven influences of the automobile and the Colonial Revival and historic preservation movements. By the 1920s New Castle was served by several improved roads that remain major transportation links today. Those included the Wilmington Road, now labeled Route 9, which traced the route of the trolley line from Wilmington to New Castle and then went on to Delaware City. In addition, the Basin Road, now Route 141, was completed in the early 1920s, and the old New Castle and Frenchtown Turnpike, now Route 273, continued to be improved. These roads connected New Castle to the Du Pont Highway, which was the spine of the state's emerging highway system.

In 1925 an automobile ferry opened across the Delaware River to connect New Castle to Pennsville, New Jersey. The ferry originally docked at the foot of Delaware Street. Later a

Townspeople and dignitaries await the arrival of the first automobile ferry to connect New Castle and New Jersey on Labor Day, 1925, at Delaware Street. This ferry location closed after a second ferry service opened at the foot of Chestnut Street the next year. *(Courtesy of New Castle Historical Society)*

Aerial view of opening day for the new ferry service captures much of the town's historic center as it looked in 1925. *(Courtesy of Hagley Museum and Library)*

competing line built a ferry slip at the foot of Chestnut Street. When the two lines merged in 1927, all ferry service was consolidated at the Chestnut Street slip. Its deteriorating wooden pilings are still visible. The ferry service brought a great number of cars and trucks to New Castle, not only from other parts of Delaware and New Jersey, but also from greater distances, especially to and from points to the south or west that were closer to New Castle than to the next available river crossing in Pennsylvania. The ferry boats remained the link from Delaware to New Jersey until the completion of the Delaware Memorial Bridge, located less than three miles to the northeast of town, in 1951.

In the age of auto tourism New Castle was on view to a large number of travelers who had never before heard of the place. Many people found the old colonial town on the Delaware River charming. It was in the context of the automobile age that the Colonial Revival, with its emphasis on historic preservation, came to New Castle and gave the town a starring role.

The consequences of the Colonial Revival movement in the United States are visible everywhere in buildings and their contents, both old and new. Historic preservationists have saved and restored structures from the colonial and federal periods, while others have incorporated elements of the Colonial Revival style into the manufacture of home furnishings and the construction of modern houses, churches, office buildings, and schools.

Scholars look back before the twentieth century to the Centennial Fair held in Philadelphia in 1876 and the Columbian Exposition World's Fair held in Chicago in 1893 as inspirations for the revival. The late nineteenth century saw the creation of genealogically based societies and the rise of a nostalgic identification with the nation's glorious early history. Some revivalists sought to emphasize colonial and Revolutionary America to teach the avalanche of immigrants from southern and eastern Europe about the values and traditions, including the architecture, of what was perceived as an earlier, simpler, more dignified, and patriotic America. In an age when homes typically were heated by radiators connected to coal-burning furnaces, it was a pleasant sentimentality to recall one's ancestors gathering around the hearths in an earlier time.

A change in aesthetic tastes also played a role in renewing respect for colonial architecture and home furnishings. Preserving the symbols of the colonial period, of the stirring days of the Revolution, and of the era of the founding of the Republic excited a generation of early-twentieth-century Americans. Twentieth-century taste for simplicity rejected the gingerbread of the late nineteenth-century styles that had once been so admired as a sign of progress. Old pre-industrial buildings that had seemed too plain in the Victorian era now attracted admiration.

New Castle, with its many pre-1840 brick buildings and history of participation in the American Revolution, was an ideal focal point for the revivalists. Here was a whole community of houses, churches, hotels, retail shops, and even a co-

Stereocard image of The Strand from Delaware Street. *(Courtesy of Delaware Historical Society)*

lonial courthouse, that captured the essence of what the revival was all about. It was, therefore, not surprising that in its second issue, published in July 1901, *House and Garden Magazine* featured a story about New Castle, illustrated with sketches by Wilson Eyre, a Philadelphia architect who constructed Colonial Revival houses for his wealthy clients.

David Boulden stands in front of his store at 25 The Strand, 1928. *(Courtesy of New Castle Historical Society)*

In 1884 the Tile House on The Strand with its date irons proclaiming the year *1687* had been demolished without a murmur, but in 1920 when the nearby Read House was threatened, an editorial in the Wilmington *Every Evening* urged that it be retained, saying "… to think of its being gutted for its treasures makes one shudder." Fortunately, the hope for the preservation of the grandest house remaining on The Strand was soon realized when Philip and Lydia Laird purchased it, undertook its restoration, and made it their home. Philip Laird was a wealthy man. His brother, William Winder Laird,

was the husband of Mary du Pont, one of Pierre S. du Pont's sisters. Philip and his brother were stockbrokers in Wilmington and handled the accounts of many wealthy clients.

The Lairds focused their attention not only on their old house but also on The Strand as a whole. Philip Laird purchased a number

Aerial view of George Read II House and Gardens after its purchase by Philip and Lydia Laird. *(Courtesy of Delaware Historical Society)*

THE BANKS BUILDING

The only building left on the wharf at the foot of Delaware Street from the time of New Castle's industrial era is the Banks Building, a rare wooden survivor of a nineteenth-century commercial structure in the vernacular Italianate style. Named for Donald Banks, a prominent resident of the town and a Trustee of the Common, this building has seen many uses since it was built in 1871 as an office and out-of-house refuge for William Jefferson. Over time it has been the custom house, marine exchange, and an office for a coal-yard and the telegraph. It is now the property of the City of New Castle.

Today the Banks Building is best remembered as a meeting place of the "senate," a group of older, retired men who gather for coffee and conversation. Over its many years of existence, the "senate" has met at various locations, most famously in the back room at White's Ice Cream Parlor, a town fixture for many years at 204 Delaware Street.

of properties on the street, including the Jefferson House Hotel (Number 5) and the Boulden grocery (Number 25). The first he converted into apartments and the latter into a residence. Laird also paid to have blacktop laid on The Strand. After the Pennsylvania Railroad abandoned its multiple sets of tracks near the river front, he aided the Trustees of the Common in creating Battery Park by buying up and removing railroad tracks and unattractive structures that lay close to The Strand.

Philip and Lydia Laird also restored the gardens adjacent to the Read House to resemble the styles of past time as imagined by modern minds. During the 1920s and 1930s their house and its garden were featured numerous times in fashionable magazines such as *House and Garden*. The Lairds demonstrated their willingness to incorporate the new into the old by building a swimming pool in the rear of the garden. Across The Strand, close to the river, they built a tennis court and a marina where their friends could tie up their yachts. The Lairds had their own friends and family and were always a bit removed from the old New Castle set, but they were a major force in the town's preservation groups and in the presentation of New Castle's heritage dating back to earliest colonial times.

In 1924 a group of New Castle's own home-grown preservationists started a tradition known as "A Day in Old New Castle." Anne Rodney Janvier organized the ladies of Immanuel Church to sell tickets to visitors eager to see the interiors of the town's leading houses and gardens on a spring Saturday. The "Day" was a great success as a fundraiser for the church and, with the exception of the years during World War II, has remained an important event into the twenty-first century. In the postwar years "A Day in Old New Castle" drew several thousand people each year to see the old town as interpreted by costumed residents in a colonial fair-like setting.

The most spectacular example of Colonial Revival restoration during the decade of the 1920s was undoubtedly Colonial Williamsburg, a project that was generously funded by John D. Rockefeller, Jr. Inspired by that example, preservationists in many American communities, including New Castle, took up the cause of saving individual buildings and creating historic museums.

In New Castle, the demise of the Tile House had become a

Hostesses for Day in Old New Castle pose in their costumes in 1953. *(Courtesy of New Castle Historical Society)*

much lamented poster child for the preservationists. They determined that their first duty must be to ensure that other iconic structures did not suffer the same fate. Their first challenge came in 1929 in the form of the Amstel House. Several of the town's leading men created the New Castle Society for the Preservation of Antiquities to restore the Amstel House and open it as a museum. The Brandywine Garden Club joined that enterprise by creating a colonial-style garden at the Amstel House. In 1934 the New Castle Society for the Preservation of Antiquities became the New Castle Historical Society, and a group of local women formed a new garden club, the Arasapha, to take over the maintenance of the house's garden.

Although not a resident of New Castle, Daniel Moore Bates took to heart the success of Williamsburg and did his best to turn the center of Delaware's colonial capital into a museum-piece, even without the support of a Rockefeller-level donor. Bates and another activist, Mary Wilson Thompson, began the Delaware Society for the Preservation of Antiquities, with the encouragement and modest support of Louise du Pont Crowninshield and her brother Henry Francis du Pont in 1937. The group took on as its first project the purchase and restoration of a small early colonial building on Third

"Map A" of the Perry, Shaw and Hepburn survey that laid out plans to re-create a Federal-era town. *(Courtesy of Delaware Historical Society)*

View of Tile House · The Strand · New Castle · Delaware
Perry, Shaw and Hepburn   and   Pope and Kruse · Associated Architects.

The Perry, Shaw and Hepburn report of 1949 envisioned re-creating the Tile House on The Strand. *(Courtesy of Delaware Historical Society)*

Street that they called the Dutch House. When the group disbanded in 1952 the Dutch House became the property of the New Castle Historical Society.

After the end of World War II, Bates continued his efforts to preserve the town's center. Again with the help of Crowninshield, he created Historic Research, Inc. (later Historic New Castle, Inc.), which engaged the Boston-based architectural firm of Perry, Shaw, and Hepburn, the architects who had planned the restoration of Williamsburg, to undertake a survey of the town and to offer a plan whereby a visit to New Castle would become a Williamsburg-like experience.

Perry, Shaw and Hepburn hired two restoration architects from Wilmington, George E. Pope and his associate Albert Kruse, along with historian Jeannette Eckman, to complete their team. They began their work in 1946 and three years later in June 1949 presented their report, replete with large illustrations, at a well-attended meeting in New Castle. The architects envisioned New Castle as a Federal-era town. Their map made clear which buildings they thought most important to preserve and noted other more recent structures such as the library on Third Street and the Opera House on Delaware Street that they thought should be removed as incongruent with the Federal-era look they envisioned. Rows of nineteenth-century townhouses would also have been sacrificed for parking areas. Most particularly, they presented a plan for removing the early-twentieth-century house that had been erected on the site of the Tile House and replacing it with a replica of the original.

Armed with the architects' survey, Bates was determined to create a wholly colonial/ Federal appearance to New Castle's central core. The town, however, never found its John D. Rockefeller, Jr. Furthermore, the architects themselves included a caution in their report. "Throughout the work of this survey, the authors … have experienced a growing conviction toward the principle of preservation rather than restoration." In that spirit they urged the people of New Castle to use "carefully considered zoning regulations" as the best way "to hold on to what they already possess." The city government took that advice and created a Board of Historic Review, composed of five members who were knowledgeable about historic architecture to pass judgment on owners' proposals to alter the façades of the buildings in the town's historical center.

Restoration and preservation, not re-creation, would have to proceed one building at a time, and most of the Victorian structures that Daniel Moore

Row of houses along Harmony Street between East Second and East Third streets would have been sacrificed to make way for a parking lot in the Perry, Shaw and Hepburn proposal.

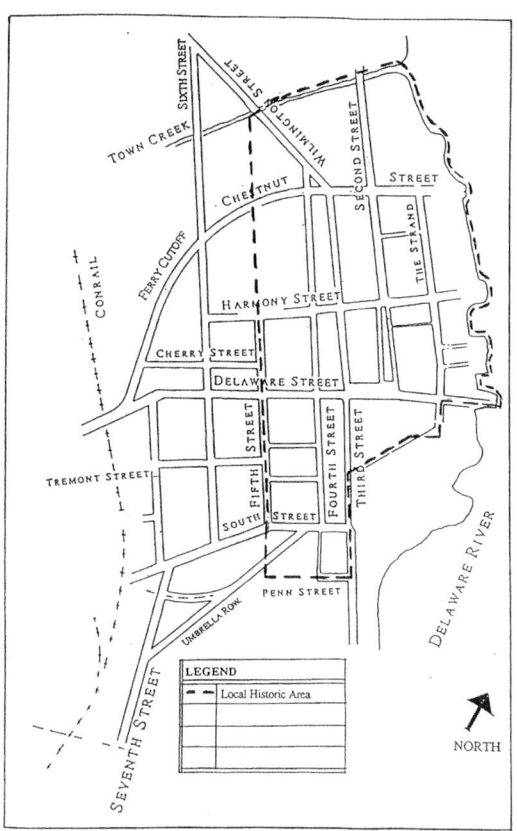

The New Castle Historic Area Commission oversees the section of town within the dotted line. *(Courtesy of City of New Castle)*

Bates would have demolished were spared. Although he failed to achieve his grand goal, Bates's community meetings succeeded in arousing the people of the town to take pride in, and to preserve, their architectural heritage. The exhaustive research into early deeds and other records undertaken by the architects and their historical consultant, Jeannette Eckman, uncovered a treasure trove of information about the history of the town and its structures that continues to be used today.

The end result of all those efforts was not a town turned into a museum fixed in one time period like Colonial Williamsburg, but a town that has continued to function as a community of residents who have homes, stores, churches, and public buildings that they use every day. In the 1960s New Castle adopted a new zoning ordinance that created the New Castle Historic Area Commission to replace the Board of Historic Review. The commission established guidelines for maintaining and restoring the exteriors of buildings based upon those set by the United States Secretary of the Interior under the National Historic Preservation Act of 1966.

The Trustees of the Common have been responsible for much of New Castle's contemporary appearance. Led by Judge Richard S. Rodney, a New Castle resident and the town's leading historian, the trustees purchased the land, wharves, and several railroad sidings to create Battery Park in 1931. They provided some of the land that became the New Castle Air Force Base during World War II, now the New Castle County Airport. The airbase was a ferrying station for all sorts of military aircraft during World War II and was a training ground for the women pilots who flew those planes to their destinations.

In the years that followed the Second World War, the area around New Castle was transformed. Where once farms had lined the way from the town southward to Delaware City, a huge oil refinery was constructed in the early 1950s. North and west of town developers built houses and strip malls on former farmland. As in other American towns, retail businesses such as grocery stores and pharmacies moved from the town center to the malls. Many of the retailers who remain in the downtown area serve the tourists who make their way to New Castle to experience a place that reflects times gone by while remaining a living community. Most residents who work outside the town commute by car.

The growth of population in the twentieth century required the construction of new schools. In 1931 William Penn School, a Colonial Revival building typical of that period, was built near the intersection of the major roads that lead into the town. The new school contained all grades from 1 through 12. By the early 1960s it could no longer accommodate all of the district's children. A much larger William Penn High School was constructed along Route 141 just in time to handle the expanding baby-boom generation. That school and others in the area are now part of an expanded district, appropriately called the Colonial School District. New Castle has become a town embedded in what can truly be called Greater New Castle County. The county courts are still in Wilmington, but county government is primarily located in an office park adjacent to the New Castle County Airport, not so far from William Penn High School.

The 1960s also saw the completion of a long-desired project: the restoration of the old courthouse, New Castle's greatest prize, into a museum that tells the story of how government arose and functioned in the early history of the First State. The courthouse restoration required the work of many hands and donors working through the New Castle Historic Buildings Commission, an agency of the State of Delaware that was chaired by a New Castle resident, Judge Daniel F. Wolcott. Delaware's first capitol building is now appropriately a state museum.

By the end of the twentieth century New Castle was unique among Delaware's communities in having become the home of museums supported by three separate historical agencies, all committed to using the best current practices of restoration, preservation, and interpretation. The New Castle Historical Society owns the Amstel and Dutch houses and also operates the 1892 library building as a museum. At her death in 1975 Lydia Laird entrusted the Read House to the Historical Society of Delaware; and the State of Delaware's Division of Historic and Cultural Affairs has responsibility for the courthouse. Those professionally managed resources are a blessing, but it is the daily efforts of the residents of New Castle and the love that they show for their homes and businesses that make this community an inspiring visual model of American life through the centuries.

INTRODUCTION TO ARCHITECTURAL STYLES IN NEW CASTLE: WHAT TO LOOK FOR

When looking at buildings most people want to know two things. First, *when was it built?* Sometimes the answer is easy and unequivocal. A structure might have a date stone; it might be easy to trace through deeds; or other historical records might be available to pinpoint the time of construction. Even if a building can be dated, it needs to be studied carefully to determine what is original and what has changed over time, a process that often requires layers and layers of research, much like peeling an onion, as well as patience, and perhaps considerable expense.

A second question asked of a building is usually: *what style is it?* This question often proves no easier to answer than the dating question. Architectural historians have created names of style categories and then listed the elements that create each style. Sometimes different experts do not use the same categories, or they divide their architectural chronologies differently. Even when they agree, the lists of elements of a style type are usually very long, with arcane vocabularies that add precision to their work but are unknown to the layperson. Moreover, many structures do not fall easily into one category. Structures may display elements from several periods or styles. Many builders and owners choose styles, or elements of styles, long after architects and trendsetters have moved on. They create vernacular architecture that reflects common, or consensual, styles of a particular time and place.

Looking at buildings in New Castle offers some challenges but many rewards. Those just learning about the town should look at a building's front, particularly its roofline, cornice, windows, and doorway, and they will be well on their way to "reading" the structure. For connoisseurs, closer study combined with historical and physical research can go on endlessly, for there is always a next layer of understanding to be uncovered. The joy of learning about buildings in one's own backyard or somewhere far away comes as much from the journey as the destination. But, beware, reading buildings is addictive.

NEW CASTLE'S ARCHITECTURAL HERITAGE

New Castle's long and rich history comes alive in the buildings and land-scape of the town. To walk through New Castle is to walk through time. In a compact space, buildings constructed over a period stretching for more than three centuries intermingle on streets first laid out by the Dutch, expanded by the English, and then enlarged by Americans.

This mingling of styles over time gives New Castle its vitality. It is a living town, not an outdoor museum frozen into one or even a few set moments. Because New Castle lives in the real world, its development reflects an ever-changing political landscape, waves of economic opportunities and stresses, changing technologies and fashions, and evolving standards of urban plan-ning. After three centuries New Castle remains a work in progress where history and architecture form an inseparable whole.

As the oldest town on the Delaware River, New Castle is the crown jewel of Delaware; and as a town that has remained small, it is accessible and invit-ing. The historical and architectural significance of its central core earned it both a National Landmark and a National Register designation from the United States Department of the Interior in 1967, which then extended the boundaries of the historic district in 1984. This expanded National Register District, encompassing nearly 500 properties in fewer than 20 square blocks, provides a memorable journey through the evolution of America's architec-

Audrey Rooney's drawing of five front doors and fanlights illustrates the variety of Georgian and Federal era styles that can still be seen in New Castle. Starting with the door of the Amstel House in the center bottom, you can trace the evolution of door surrounds from the heavier Georgian emphasis on classical pilasters and pediments to the lighter Federal look that used larger fanlights and sidelights. *(Courtesy of New Castle Historical Society)*

tural types and styles over time. Grand high-style houses of the affluent stand side by side with the medium-sized houses of the middle class and the smaller-sized less embellished but solid houses of the working class. Architect-designed structures intermingle with pattern-book and vernacular styles from eighteenth-century Georgian to the bungalows and Colonial Revivals of the twentieth century.

Frontier New Castle: Edge of Empire

Before we consider New Castle as it is today, we should pause for remembrance—for the memory of what no longer stands. The older the place, the longer is the opportunity for loss. Sometimes buildings are intentionally destroyed, as old makes way for new because of changing tastes or economic circumstances. Sometimes buildings are lost through natural disasters such as fires or floods, and sometimes buildings are not created to last forever.

New Castle's trail of loss begins with the buildings of its first fifty years or so, its frontier period—whether private houses, government structures, or churches—all but one have vanished from our view. What doomed the structures from that turbulent period was not the many transfers of political power, usually accompanied by religious or linguistic change, but rather what they were made of: wood. From Fort Casimir to William Penn's first courthouse, early New Castle was a world of wood, usually unseasoned or "green" wood that lacked strength and durability. As in all frontier communities, the first buildings were erected hurriedly with inadequate materials that were not designed to stand the test of time.

In the seventeenth century, trees, indeed forests of hardwoods, stood close by, but New Castle, situated in a flat area of slow-moving streams, lacked a source of strong running water to power a sawmill. For early New Castilians, transforming that forest resource, first into logs and then into squared timbers, boards, or roof shingles, required great manual labor. The earliest tools settlers would have used were the ax and adze. The first mention of a sawmill comes in 1664, but that term would have meant a saw set within a frame powered at each end by a man. One man stood in a pit while the other stood atop the log or squared timber. Up and down the saw would go, cutting only on the downward motion. This slow, labor-intensive process limited local production. Timber could be brought in by boat, but few, if any, water-powered sawmills existed in the Delaware Valley until late in the seventeenth century. Kilns, or ovens, for drying lumber also came later. Indeed, the kiln-dried, standardized sizes of lumber we know today date only from the second half of the nineteenth century.

In comparison to other materials, though, timber and lumber supply seemed positively abundant. The old assertion that bricks arrived in New Castle, as in other early trading centers, as ballast in European ships has largely been discredited. Fort Casimir had a brick kiln, the records tell us, by the late 1650s, but it was a small, rudimentary affair, producing only enough bricks to build chimneys. Then the brickmaker died, and the kiln remained cold for a time, forcing settlers to beg that bricks and other supplies be sent to them. Bricks could be obtained from a greater distance, most particularly from New Amsterdam/New York or further up the Hudson River, but the Dutch settlement on the Delaware was initially expected to be as self-sufficient as possible; it was to be a net exporter, not importer. A large commercial kiln capable of supplying the quantities of bricks needed for house construction began only in the 1680s on the far-west side of New Castle in the area of Fifth and South streets.

In the town's early years, roof tiles, nails, hardware, glass, and other building materials had to be imported to build the wood structures. Dutch settlers up the Hudson River made red pantiles, or roof tiles, by the 1650s, and some were brought to New Castle, but they would have been used only on steeply pitched roofs. Most early New Castle roofs were covered with the more readily accessible hand-cut wood shingles. Nails and hardware were produced locally at an early date by blacksmiths working small forges to heat, hammer, snip, and shape iron into nails, hardware, and other household needs, although once again charcoal for the smiths' forges was sometimes in short supply. Glass remained the most difficult product to obtain. The Dutch made the first window glass in America, but for a long period most glass had to be imported from Europe, making it a rare, expensive construction element. Philadelphia's first glasshouse, as a glassworks was then called, was started in 1683, but within a short period of time the enterprise failed.

The reliance on wood doomed the earliest buildings of seventeenth-century New Castle to impermanence. That loss took with it any opportunity to study, at least from above ground, how a small, multicultural, polyglot population—indeed the most multicultural town in all of seventeenth-century America—shared their construction techniques and aesthetics. Fortunately, some sense of New Castle in its first few decades can be gleaned from a few early travelers' accounts. Each provides a verbal snapshot in time, but their reports often seem contradictory because the town's prosperity and the size of its population ebbed and surged depending on economic realities, ranging from weather patterns to larger geopolitical and economic forces.

In general, it is fair to say that the town grew slowly. Extant land records show that lots were bought and sold as they became available, and many individuals owned multiple properties. Yet land transactions never reached a pace of speculative frenzy. Over time more and larger wood houses with brick chimneys and wood or tile roofs replaced the original small log structures, and the original large lots, a city-block deep, began to be subdivided into the pattern of lot sizes you see today.

Before William Penn's arrival, the two largest or grandest houses stood along Harmony Street between The Strand and present-day Third Street. Each was built probably in the decade between 1662 and 1672 on land first owned by the chief administrators of the Dutch colony and then by important citizens serving in the Duke of York's government.

One house stood on Harmony Street just above Second Street, directly across from the blockhouse built to replace Fort Casimir that is now the location of Immanuel Church. No description of the house exists beyond its size: it was the only space in New Castle large enough to accommodate a Quaker meeting in 1672 that attracted most of the town's population to hear George Fox, founder of The Society of Friends, who was travelling and preaching in the English colonies. The second house stood on the north side of Harmony Street just above The Strand. It was built of brick, using mortar made from local sand and lime burned from oyster shells. Low elliptical arches of yellow bricks spanned the tops of all the windows and doors. Its hand-hewn timbers testified to the period before sawmills. Benjamin Ferris, Delaware's first historian, remembered seeing the house as late as the 1780s.

Building a Colonial Town

When William Penn became proprietor in 1682, he commissioned Thomas Holme to make a map that could be used to attract settlers to his lands, for he wanted his colonies to be both religiously tolerant and personally remunerative. The major portion of the map provides a detailed layout of Philadelphia and its near environs, while New Castle is shown only in broadest sketch form. At best this map suggests a settlement rather than a delineation of the town as it then appeared. It provides, alas, merely a sense of the size of the town, but nothing else. Neither the layout, nor scale, nor style of buildings should be taken literally.

The Tile House One building believed to date from Penn's first decade of ownership did survive for almost 200 years and became a favorite subject for both scholars and artists. That structure came to be called the Tile House because of the Dutch-type small yellow brick, called tiles by the English, used on its street façade. The building has been dated to 1687 on the basis of date irons anchored into the façade. While not built until after the period of Dutch colonial ownership, paintings and photographs of the Tile House show a Dutch-style building with steep roof and stepped gable façade made of small apricot-colored bricks and marked by distinctive fenestration and shallow niches. Its uniqueness sets it apart from the other structures recorded by Benjamin Henry Latrobe and his assistants in their town survey made at the beginning of the nineteenth century. Although the Tile House may be the

Tile House as it looked in 1804-05 in the Latrobe Survey. *(Courtesy of Delaware Public Archives)*

only recorded step-gabled façade in New Castle, but a number of examples of similar design and dating can be found in pictures of New York from that period.

Time did not treat the Tile House kindly. It passed through a variety of owners and received numerous repairs, including a major rebuilding, yet over time it lost its status on the town's best merchant street and became so deteriorated that it was an eyesore to its neighbors. In 1884 it was demolished, but the old building did not go easily. Apparently its

Watercolor of the Tile House in decline, painted by Edward Williams Clay, 1822. *(Courtesy of New Castle Historical Society)*

Photograph of a substantially modified Tile House awaiting demolition. *(Courtesy of New Castle Historical Society)*

walls proved to be so solid that it required dynamite to bring them down. Over time the derelict structure became venerable in old timers' memories, and it continues to be revered as the town's most beloved "lost" structure.

While we can lament all of the losses of frontier New Castle, so much remains from the period of the Penn family's proprietorship forward that New Castle can truly be seen as a treasure-trove of architectural riches spanning three centuries. To start with the earliest building that still exists today means to start with the building at 32 East Third Street, called the Dutch House, a building with a long, convoluted history.

The Dutch House This charming, small dwelling has attracted great attention over the years, with some authors waxing eloquent over its quaint, romantic, even fairy-tale-like qualities. Yet the house remained shrouded in mystery, stubbornly refusing to reveal its full history until 2003, when a detailed documentary and physical study was completed for the New Castle Historical Society to use as the basis for a full restoration of the exterior.

The preponderance of evidence demonstrates that, despite its name, the dwelling does not date back to the period of the Dutch colony. Land along

The Dutch House.

Third Street did not begin to be sold until the 1670s during the Duke of York period. In the 1680s only two log houses existed there, including one on the Dutch House lot, which was owned by a carpenter. Scarcity of records make it impossible to assign a precise date to when the wood-frame Dutch House replaced the log dwelling, but the best estimate based on those records would be in the late 1690s. That would place the construction of the Dutch House at a time when the pace of development in the block of Third Street facing today's Green began to accelerate. Subdivision of properties into smaller lots and the construction of the block's first brick house, now gone, marked the transition to an urbanizing area populated by artisans.

Many have believed that the first owner of the Dutch House was of Dutch ancestry and that the house reflected his heritage. Deed records suggest such an assumption is highly unlikely, but that in no way diminishes the significance of the dwelling as an example of New Castle's melting pot of cultures. The Dutch House should be understood as a hybrid. Its frame construction combines both English and Dutch building techniques and technologies available around 1700. Like many buildings of the early-eighteenth-century Delaware Valley, the house cannot be pigeonholed into a stylistic category. It is a unique amalgam.

As the oldest surviving structure in town, the Dutch House has a long and complex story that serves as a caution against taking a building at face value. Assuming that an old building has maintained the same appearance over time is often wrong—a lesson to be kept in mind when looking at houses far more recent than the Dutch House. Over the years the Dutch

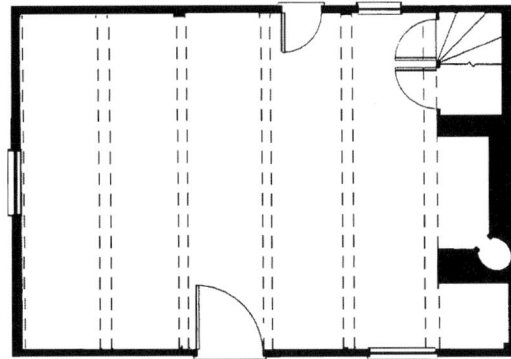

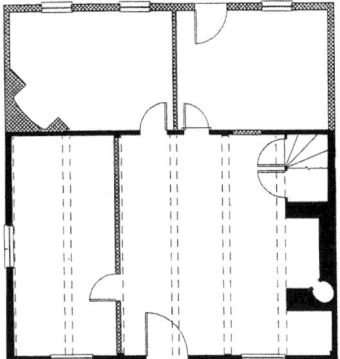

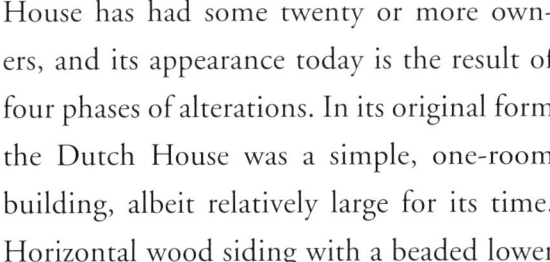

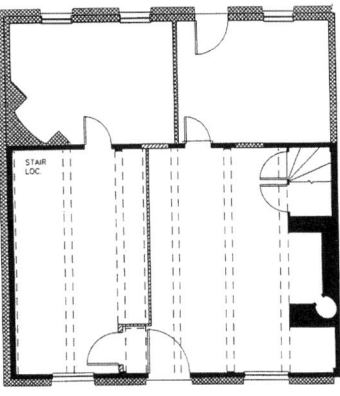

Dutch House floor plans showing its evolution from a one-room "hall" through the expansion of space, creation of separate rooms, and changes in doorways over the course of the eighteenth century. *(Courtesy of New Castle Historical Society)*

House has had some twenty or more owners, and its appearance today is the result of four phases of alterations. In its original form the Dutch House was a simple, one-room building, albeit relatively large for its time. Horizontal wood siding with a beaded lower edge covered the frame on the outside, while inside were plastered walls and exposed ceiling beams. A large fireplace stood at the north end with a winder-stair fitted into the back corner of the chimney bay leading to a shallow loft space. Sometimes called a "hall" plan because of its roots in the world of late medieval Europe, it was the most common house form of the region at the beginning of the 1700s. The house's original plan meant that all family activities—eating, working, and sleeping—took place in the same space.

Changes to the Dutch House spanned 125 or so years as owners chose how to expand and reconfigure the interior to suit evolving needs and tastes. First came the creation of separate rooms so that a family could cook, sleep, and socialize in different spaces. Room usage then changed more than once as social status and concepts of fashion altered with time. The kitchen, for example, became first its own room in the front of the house as befitted the room of central family focus. Then as concepts of gentility changed, so did the place of the kitchen. It moved to the back of the house, flip-flopping with the now more important parlor. By the 1820s the original one-room house with storage loft had become a dwelling with four rooms on the first floor and more rooms upstairs. Time brought changes to the exterior too, including the addition of a basement, the re-siding of three walls with brick, and the alteration of roofline to the steep overhang seen today. The wrapping of the exterior walls with brick helps account for the survival of the town's earliest extant building.

During the next century the Dutch House continued to pass through many hands, and by the 1930s it was a deteriorating rental property in danger of going the way of the Tile House. Fortunately, a preservation group was organized to save the oldest known house in New Castle, and it is now a property of the New Castle Historical Society. The Dutch House and the adjoining garden created when the house was saved are open to the public. The first surprise when visiting the house is that you have to step down to enter. That was not always the case, but street re-grading in the early nineteenth century altered the way the house sits on the land.

Building an English Town

The evolution of the Dutch House did not occur in a vacuum. Rather it serves as a mirror of the growth and development of New Castle as it became slowly but inevitably English in character. First came military control, followed by British law and government, new waves of immigration and religions, the introduction of the English language, a position within the English mercantile system, and, most visibly, English architectural styles and technologies.

Beginning in the 1660s, New Castle developed as an English-looking town. This occurred during an era of great change in architectural styles in England and in her colonies. It was a time marked by the transformation in English high-style architecture away from the Elizabethan style toward classicism with its emphasis on restrained elegance, symmetry, and mathematical precision. The leaders of this new style were Inigo Jones (1573-1652) and Christopher Wren (1632-1723). Inigo Jones is best remembered for introducing the refined classical elements pioneered by the Italian architect Andrea Palladio (1518-1580) in the previous century to the construction of palatial buildings in England. Christopher Wren, a mathematician by training, designed college buildings and London's Saint Paul's Cathedral, as well as a host of small, classically inspired churches built in London to replace those destroyed in the fire of 1666. The work of those men is reflected in the later emergence of styles in America that we call Georgian and later Federal.

The term *Georgian* refers to the eighteenth-century kings of England named George, beginning with George I who came to the throne in 1714. After about 1720, pattern books and new professional architects carried this English style of classical architecture from London to the towns and countryside of Great Britain and on to her colonies, including those on the Delaware River. Even before then, Penn himself helped bring the architectural style of London townhouses after the Great Fire to his new colonies. He had a plan for a "beginners" house included in his advertising to attract settlers. Called the Penn Plan or the Quaker Plan by architectural historians, the design can be seen as part of the continuum that we broadly characterize as Georgian.

What characterized a building as Georgian was an exterior formality and symmetry based upon mathematical calculations of proportions. The size and placement of windows and doors were key elements in Georgian architecture, as was façade ornamentation, all derived from ancient Roman forms. The popularity of Georgian architecture was due, at least in part, to its accessibility to almost all levels of society. The rich might have elaborate pilasters and cornices based on the classical orders, but even the dwellings of the working class could have some ornamentation around the door. Here was a style that could accommodate public and private buildings for a king or for humble workers.

At first slowly, and then with ever-greater acceleration, Penn's colonies became Georgian in look and feel. The Georgian style suited the building, and in some cases rebuilding, of New Castle as it had already been laid out. The trail of that "Georgianization" process in New Castle can be traced through three buildings dating between 1707 and 1738, the years when the town moved from colonial outpost to colonial capital. Individually each of these buildings retains an exterior that provides core visual integrity; collectively they embody most of the defining characteristics of Georgian architecture. Over time the buildings fall into a stylistic continuum of scale and ornamentation from smaller and plainer to larger and more elaborate, from restrained to elegant, and from relatively tentative in execution of design to skillful presentation.

New Castle Presbyterian Church Begin on Second Street with the New Castle Presbyterian Church. The congregation cannot claim to own the oldest surviving religious structure in town, but they do have the oldest church in its original form. The church you see today was built in two sections between 1707 and 1712, with only a seam in the exterior walls to demark the sections. As old as their church is, the congregation has always traced its roots back even further, to the beginning of the Dutch colony on the Delaware and the religious services held within Fort Casimir. After the English captured the colony, Scottish Presbyterianism slowly replaced Dutch Reformed, but since both derived from a similar Calvinistic tradition they had much in common. The church built by New Castle's Presbyterians in brick to replace an earlier wooden Dutch church exhibits many architectural features of the early Georgian period. Townspeople, and all those who admire colonial architecture, can rejoice that this building still stands, but its survival was not always assured.

Since Second Street did not exist when the Presbyterian Church was built, except as the edge of the Market Plaine, what we see from that street today was originally the rear of the building at the rear of the property. For nearly a century congregants would have walked up a path from The Strand, an approach that remains accessible today. In time, changing tastes and needs began to catch up with the building. In 1803 a balcony was completed to accommodate a growing congregation, and in the middle of that century

New Castle Presbyterian Church, from the Latrobe Survey. *(Courtesy of Delaware Public Archives)*

the church underwent a series of interior and exterior repairs and changes for structural and aesthetic reasons. Roof, windows, floors, and pews were replaced, and venetian blinds were added inside, while outside coats of plaster covered the brick walls. With the opening of Second Street, the entrance of the church

This photograph captures both the close proximity and the vast differences in architectural styles of the eighteenth- and nineteenth-century churches. *(Courtesy of New Castle Historical Society)*

was moved to that side of the building, and a brick wall was added to mark the property line. Finally, though, no amount of repairs or rearrangement could make the church sufficiently large or modern for the congregation.

The nearly 150-year-old church seemed old-fashioned compared to the new Gothic styles popular in religious architecture of the mid-nineteenth century. Fortunately, when the congregation built a new church of brownstone in 1854, the old brick building was not torn down; it was merely relegated to secondary status as the Sunday School.

When the neo-Gothic, brownstone church, in turn, began to show the ravages of age a cen-

Watercolor of New Castle Presbyterian Church by Frank Soltesz, early 1970s. *(Courtesy of Robert and Joan Appleby)*

tury later, aesthetic sensibilities had again changed. With the demolition of the structurally unsound brownstone building, it was time for the original church, having now achieved a venerable status, to reclaim its place as the center of Presbyterian worship in New Castle. By 1950 the old had become new again, or at least as close to the 1707–12 look as possible. The brownstone church was replaced by a colonial-style education building.

Some have called the Presbyterian Church small and simple, but for its time it was neither small nor simple. Now, as then, it might best be characterized as elegantly restrained. On the Second Street side, four round-headed windows, each with a brick keystone in the relieving arch, and a double door with fanlight manifest its early Georgian style, as does the water table at ground level and the brick stringcourse above the windows. All of those elements are decorative, but in a modest way. The gambrel roof with jerkinhead or clipped gable ends and a wide but plain cove cornice add to the church's Georgian appearance. The vestibule, with its homage to the roofline of the church, is a 1950 addition. The cupola also dates from 1950, recreated to look as it had in the Latrobe survey of 1805. Perhaps the best way to appreciate the longevity of New Castle Presbyterian Church is to walk around it and look at the brick, which records all the centuries of changes. On The Strand side, note particularly the repairs that closed in the space where the original door stood.

8 The Strand, from the Latrobe Survey. *(Courtesy of Delaware Public Archives)*

8 The Strand A second example is found at 8 The Strand. Built between circa 1700 and 1730, this three-bay, gable-end house reflects the relatively simple, unadorned façade and imperfect proportioning typical of the early period. The front door is set within a slightly recessed frame of simple molding and is topped by a plain glass transom. The door itself is a replacement, but its simplicity of eight raised panels maintains the façade's integrity, as do the two-panel shutters on the first-floor windows. The windows are perhaps the most interesting element of the façade. The style of the windows with small twelve-over-twelve panes of glass held in sash frames by pieces of wood called muntins are period appropriate for an early Georgian house, yet they appear out of scale. Their disproportionately large size may suggest the taste of the owner but more likely reflects the level of training of the builders. Such indi-

8 The Strand today.

viduality gives this house its particular charm. The chimney placement is also early Georgian. Its location at the rear of the gable wall farthest from the door was designed as a heat-saving feature. The original house had two rooms on each floor, but over time 8 The Strand has been expanded to include an addition in the rear, a side porch, and a dormer. Still the house projects its Georgian origins.

Number 8 The Strand, like its slightly later neighbor at Number 6, seems to sit high on the street. Originally both stood at ground level, but the early-nineteenth-century re-grading of New Castle's streets lowered The Strand in front of those two buildings so much that steps had to be added. That change allows visitors today to see the brick relieving arches that carried the weight of basement openings for Number 6.

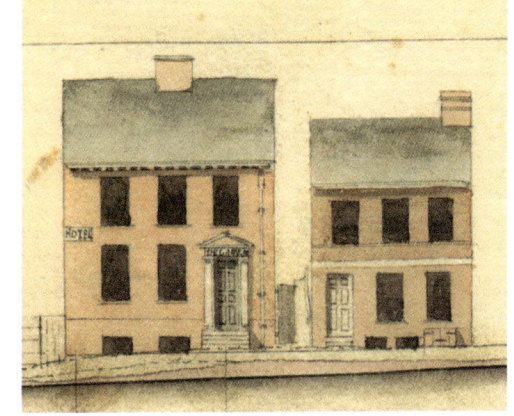

Detail of the Latrobe Survey's "Section of Front Street" shows how the street level would change for 6 and 8 The Strand, which explains their needs for front steps today. *(Courtesy of Delaware Public Archives)*

The Amstel House Our third Georgian example at 2 East Fourth Street was built a few years later than 6 The Strand. Here is an outstanding example of colonial architecture, not just for New Castle but for all of the colonies. John Finney, a doctor and prominent town citizen, acquired the property in 1738 and soon began to build a grand, imposing house that dominated its sur-

The Amstel House at 2 East Fourth Street.

roundings. Here Georgian architectural features abound: the water table at street level; a stringcourse, stepped on the Delaware Street side and straight across the façade; and the pedimented gable facing Fourth Street. Interestingly, the broad gable end is turned to the front, an unusual but not unique house placement that fell out of favor by the mid-eighteenth century. Other notable Georgian features include brickwork in the Flemish and English bond patterns and the great double cove cornice.

For all of its imposing size, the main portion of the Amstel House is essentially a big box with three rooms on both first and second floors plus a central hallway. Befitting the taste and pocketbook of its first owner, this main section boasted an interior with fine wood moldings and paneling plus eight-foot ceilings, unusually high for this period of construction. The break in the roof line and the step in the stringcourse clearly demark the division between the main house and the kitchen wing, with its lower ceilings and lack of detailing suitable for the servants who lived and worked there.

Only one element is not in keeping with all of the Amstel House's original features, and that is the front entry. The wooden door surround with its elaborate combination of pilasters topped by a pediment and enriched

Amstel House doorway.

by classical elements, including a keystone-topped fanlight, stands out as a later enhancement. That first alteration in the house came in the decade just before the American Revolution, perhaps about the time Dr. Finney died and the house became a high-end rental property. The house's location near to the courthouse made it desirable. First Nicholas Van Dyke, a wealthy lawyer and political leader during the Revolutionary War, lived there while governor, followed by his son-in-law, Kensey Johns, a rising lawyer. Van Dyke was a wealthy man who owned a number of farms south of New Castle but, like many of the period, chose not to own a house in town since he needed an urban base only when the assembly and the courts were in session.

The nineteenth century brought multiple changes in ownership of the Amstel House as well as alterations to the fabric of the building. Changes in the brickwork can be seen clearly along the Delaware Street side, indicating changes in the use of openings as doors and windows. Changes in ownership and use also mark the building's history. For a time it slipped in prominence, and its resi-

Side view of the Amstel House with its distinctive Georgian architectural features of stringcourse, beltcourse, and relieving arches.

Restored parlor of the Amstel House. *(Courtesy of New Castle Historical Society)*

dents included commercial tenants. About 1905, a new owner commissioned a local architect and artist, Laussat Richter Rogers, to modernize the house within the new aesthetic called Colonial Revival. The current name of the house comes from that era of paying homage to a past more idealized than real.

A twentieth-century owner named his eighteenth-century house after the river that flows through Amsterdam to honor the seventeenth-century ancestry of the property's first known owner.

In 1929 when the Amstel House stood in danger, a group of concerned citizens organized to raise the money to buy the property and begin its restoration. The original organization reincorporated itself as the New Castle Historical Society in 1934. The house today stands as a testament to the care and restoration practices that organization has practiced for over seventy-five years. Visitors today can get as close as possible to Dr. Finney's original fine house as it stood in pre-Revolutionary New Castle.

The Federal Style in a New Nation

In the years before and during the American Revolution increased public uncertainty and anxiety slowed development in New Castle almost to a halt. Another phase of growth had to wait until optimism returned with the new Republic. But while construction stopped, architectural styles continued to evolve. The public and private buildings that survive in the town from about 1780 into the 1830s reflect a new architectural environment that did not so much break with the past Georgian style as seek to refine it. Because by time this style fit so neatly with the formative years of the new nation, it came to be called Federal, though it had its roots back in the old Mother Country. Americans essentially borrowed the late-eighteenth-century British style called Adam after its chief exponent, Robert Adam (1728-1792), and then adapted that style to the new nation's own needs and abilities. The Federal style perfectly suited urban centers, like New Castle, that were growing in size and expectations.

Houses remained essentially boxes, or a descending series from a main box to one, or more, smaller service-wing boxes in the rear designed to fit narrow town lots. Strict symmetry in the placement of doors and windows continued from the Georgian era, but houses in the new style displayed greater sophistication of architectural details and mastery of construction techniques. Federal structures are often described as lighter, more elegant, more horizontally proportioned, and more delicate in both exterior and interior appearance as compared to their predecessors. The progression from what is identified as Georgian to what is identified as Federal was incremental. Indeed, some owners and builders retained "Georgian" elements throughout the Federal period and beyond, allowing future generations endless opportunities to debate style names for individual houses.

Federal-style architecture requires particular attention in New Castle because of the style's significance for the town's built environment. It is the style most associated with the town, and, indeed, its popularity lasted far longer in New Castle than in most other urban areas along the East Coast. Some of the town's finest houses are Federal in style, and we will look briefly at just four of them. Yet for every high-style building, many more were built for a growing middle class and for laborers, as a few additional examples will illustrate. Once you become familiar with the characteristics of the Federal style, you will see its influence on buildings extending into modern time.

The four impressive Federal-style houses that we will consider are all near the Green, the best location for the four lawyer-owners. Collectively they trace the evolving Federal style in New Castle. For example, compared with the Amstel House, a high-style house of the colonial period, the detailing of door surrounds and fanlights became more elaborate and intricate, with particular emphasis placed on classical forms and styles. Windows also changed.

They became larger, as the panes of glass also became bigger because of improved techniques in glassmaking. New window shapes can also be seen in New Castle, particularly the Palladian style, which featured a set of three windows: a tall central sash arched at the top and flanked on both sides by smaller rectangular sashes. Brick remained the primary building material for higher-end structures, which often also used stone for lintels, keystones, and sills as well as iron for railings and even balconies. In the Federal style rooflines were often lowered, with balustrades atop the most elaborate examples. The Federal style also favored a flatter façade than had Georgian style, so projecting elements such as water tables and stringcourses disappeared.

The Federal style changed interiors as well as exteriors. Upper-end houses often had more rooms and a greater variety of room uses than did comparable Georgian-style houses. Rooms became larger in length, width, and height, except, of course, for those in the service areas and servants' quarters. It is in a house's interior that the influence of Robert Adam is best seen. In many rooms, plaster replaced wood paneling, and decorative ornamentation in both plaster and wood was applied to ceilings, mantels, and walls. Wood moldings became more elaborate, with reeding, fluting, and other types of carving that allowed yet one more way for craftsmen to showcase their skills and for owners to assert their taste and affluence. Much of this ornamentation reflected the renewed interest in designs from antiquity that Adam championed.

2 East Third Street, built by Kensey Johns. From the Latrobe Survey. *(Courtesy of Delaware Public Archives)*

The Kensey Johns House An introduction to Federal New Castle begins with the house at 2 East Third Street. Known as the Kensey Johns House for its first owner, the main house dates from 1789-90, clearly placing it in the Federal era, yet by style it might best be called Late Georgian-Early Federal since it features elements of both. When he built the house, Johns

The Kensey Johns House today.

was a lawyer with high aspirations. He obviously understood the significance of location by choosing one of the most prominent sites in town, adjacent to the then seat of county government. Fortunately for scholars, Johns left an unusually full record of the design and construction of his house—and it was his house. Like many well-read men of the time, such as Thomas Jefferson, Johns served as his own architect. He drew, and saved, all of the seven plans he rejected before he settled on a two-story brick house with two rooms on each floor and a side hallway. A local carpenter, who served as what today would be called a general contractor, then carried out Johns's plan under the owner's oversight. The end product stands as testimony to the knowledge and good taste of Johns and the skills of local carpenters, masons, and members of other building trades. In 1795 Johns added a single-story addition on the front of the original house to serve as his office as well as a kitchen wing in the rear to replace the original basement kitchen.

The main block of the house stands on raised basement walls of dressed stone, an added expense, but one that gives the house a greater sense of height and quality. Yet the house remains a simple box with a gabled roof finished by an unornamented cornice. The front door stands recessed about a foot within a paneled entry, which is, in turn, crowned by a modest and tasteful surround copied from a Georgian architectural book published in 1757. Gently tapering pilasters are topped by a carved frieze and pediment.

The Kensey Johns House doorway.

No glass transom or fanlight adorns the entry, although these will be seen in later Federal examples in New Castle. The subdued door treatment draws the eye to the stone window sills and lintels, which feature keystones on the first floor. The interior, not accessible to the public, contains fine wood paneling that was also based on the architectural book of 1757.

Kensey Johns's house served him well during his long life and career, where he spent some thirty years as the Chief Justice of Delaware. The year before he died in 1848 at the venerable age of 89, he held a reception in his home for Henry Clay during Clay's unsuccessful bid for the American presidency. Indeed, the Kensey Johns House continues to wear its historic significance well, retaining the restrained elegance that Johns sought when he drew his house plans in the first years of the new Republic.

Nicholas Van Dyke, Jr., House In 1799 a new house rose at 400 Delaware Street, directly facing the side of the Amstel House. Built in full Federal style by Nicholas Van Dyke, Jr., this imposing two-and-a-half-story house has all of the design elements appropriate to an owner of wealth and sophistication. Built of brick in the Flemish Bond pattern from cornice line down to the sidewalk, the front of the house is a full five bays wide and boasts a large, three-bay central section that projects slightly forward and is topped by a pedimented center gable. This façade design element places the Van Dyke House in the top tier of high-style Federal-style houses in America. Pilasters and a pediment in simple but delicate classical form surround the recessed

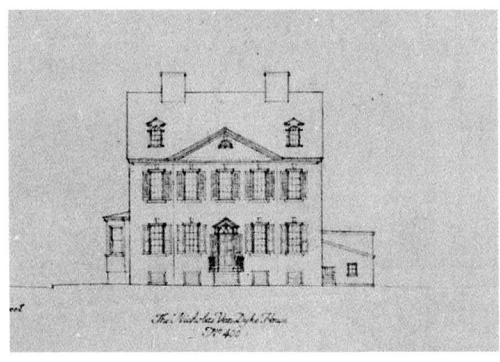

400 Delaware Street, built by Nicholas Van Dyke, Jr., from Perry, Shaw and Hepburn survey, late 1940s. *(Courtesy of New Castle Historical Society)*

doorway and fanlight, while ornamental blocks called modillions carry the classical motif into the cornice. Stone keystones, the sills on all of the façade's windows, and a semicircular fan opening within the pediment provide visual contrast to the brick. Dormers in the gable roof have arched windows and pediments.

The interior continues the same level of sophistication as the exterior, with carved woodwork, marble fireplace surrounds, and mantels decorated with small molded pieces, often called composition ornaments. Since the house at 400 Delaware Street remains in private ownership, we'll let Nicholas Van Dyke, Jr., describe the interior. His house, he said

Nicholas Van Dyke, Jr., House today.

in an advertisement, had four rooms plus hall on the first floor, "all done in the modern stile," plus five rooms on the second and four on the third. Van Dyke also noted the ample garden behind the house. Subsequent changes made to the house over time have not intruded on Van Dyke's imposing façade.

Nicholas Van Dyke, Jr., was born in New Castle and spent much of his youth living in the Amstel House. After attending Princeton College he read law with his brother-in-law Kensey Johns. The two men shared interests in law, government, and architecture, but whereas Johns built but one house, Van Dyke built or expanded four in the years 1794-1820. He, above all others in New Castle, deserves to be remembered as the gentleman architect of the Federal style. Like his father, Van Dyke also served in government, in the Delaware General Assembly, and in both houses of the United States Congress. Over the years he and his family moved five times, always seeking to create houses of good taste and quality. All one needs to do is look at 400 Delaware, his first house, and 300 Delaware Street, his last, to appreciate his architectural achievements.

The George Read II House Even before Nicholas Van Dyke, Jr., started his first house, another son of a towering Revolutionary era figure in Delaware began his own building project a few blocks away. George Read, Jr., wanted to make an architectural statement with his house at 42 The Strand. He aimed to create, in his own words, "the grandest house" in Delaware, one comparable to the highest-style houses of Philadelphia. Read's only impediment was money, or at least ready cash. Because his purse often proved inadequate to the costs associated with his grand design, the construction phase stretched from 1797 to 1804.

Read, like Johns and Van Dyke, Jr., had the education, affluence, and interest to be a gentleman architect. With help from family members in Philadelphia, he worked through a series of designs before choosing the version we see today. Read's written record of construction details, including the cost of materials and his own monetary woes, were saved and are preserved by the Delaware Historical Society, which has owned the property since 1975. Read chose Peter Crouding, a carpenter-builder from Philadelphia, to execute his design and to deal with suppliers and other workers. Crouding was no ordinary carpenter; he belonged to the organization of master craftsmen known as the Carpenters' Company of Philadelphia. Although not without its frustrations and frictions, the result of that collaboration is a magnificent five-bay-wide brick house of twenty-two rooms and 14,000

square feet, a house that displays many high-style elements in that seemingly impossible combination of mass and delicacy.

A raised basement emphasizes the Read House's height, which carries the eye from sidewalk level up beyond the roof dormers to the balustrade with its urn-shaped finials, which runs the full length of the house between the towering double chimneys at each end. The central bay clearly dominates the façade. An oversize mahogany door stands recessed within panels flanked by full-length sidelights and fluted pilasters with capitals, whose job it is

George Read II House, 42 The Strand. From the Latrobe Survey. *(Courtesy of Delaware Public Archives)*

to support the keystone-topped and elegantly detailed arched moldings that surround a fanlight. The fanlight is particularly large, spanning both door and sidelights. Above the door sits a large Palladian window with carved woodworking and rounded iron balcony. Other high-style elements include stone sills and lintels, the latter with keystones on the first and second floors, which sup-

George Read II House today. *(Courtesy of Delaware Historical Society)*

port oversized sash windows with large six-over-six panels of glass, a boxed cornice with modillions, and beautifully detailed pedimented gable dormers with arch-headed windows.

The interior of the George Read II House is open to visitors. It continues Read's love for rich ornamentation, which seems to have had few limitations beyond his pocketbook. Oversize mahogany doors, elaborately carved moldings, including a gilt sunburst in the fanlight over the doors between the two parlors, jib windows leading outside from the back parlor, carved hallway arches, and a second Palladian window on the stair landing only begin to spell out the house's interior richness. Molded plasterwork and ornamented mantels as well as a palate of striking wall colors from salmon to verdigris confirm the owner's good taste and design sensibilities. Imagine what lawyer Read's

Restored back parlor of George Read II House. *(Courtesy of Delaware Historical Society)*

This view from Delaware Street shows the houses that brothers-in-law Kensey Johns and Nicholas Van Dyke, Jr., built across the street from each other. The Johns House (2 East Third Street) predates the Van Dyke House (300 Delaware Street) by thirty years.

clients must have thought while waiting in the imposing hallway before entering his office, which was located in the room to the right of the front door.

Kensey Johns Van Dyke House If a brief journey through the maturation of the Federal style in New Castle began at the corner of Third and Delaware, it ends just across the street at 300 Delaware Street. Now brothers-in-law Kensey Johns and Nicholas Van Dyke, Jr., could live beside each other. Compare this house, Van Dyke's last, with his earlier house up one block. The differences in massing and style are noticeable. In about 1820, when Van Dyke, Jr., was in his fifties, he built a very different house from the one he had built thirty years earlier. His new two-and-a-half-story brick townhouse seems on the one hand to be plainer, yet on the other hand more subtly sophisticated than his earlier house.

The design of the house at 300 Delaware Street incorporates elements of several newer styles called variously Regency and Classical Revival. The doorway, for example, contains many of those elements found at the Read House: a recessed door flanked by sidelights and topped by a large fanlight. But here there is no elaborately constructed and carved surround. It is all simply set within a brick opening with a plain brick relieving arch at the top. The cornice manifests the same understated approach. It is corbelled brick but laid in a stylish dog-tooth pattern.

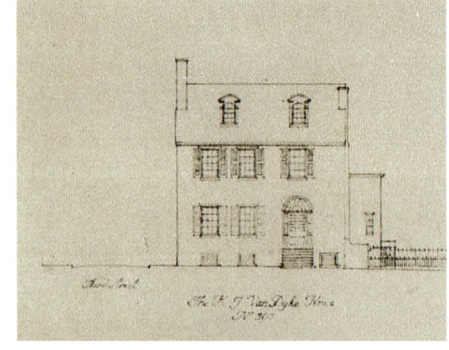

300 Delaware Street, known as the Kensey Johns Van Dyke House, from Perry, Shaw and Hepburn survey of the late 1940s. *(Courtesy of New Castle Historical Society)*

Window details of Kensey Johns Van Dyke House at 300 Delaware Street include incised "bull's eyes" on marble lintels and shutters ornamented by a pattern of carved concentric circles.

The front door and first-floor shutters on the façade are unusually paneled. Instead of plain raised panels, Van Dyke chose to have the panels carved with a series of concentric rectangles. All panels on the shutters are horizontal, while the door has both horizontally and vertically placed panels. The marble lintels above the windows on the façade have ends decorated with double incised circles or "bull's eyes." At roof level rounded windows are set within a fully decorated surround topped by an arched pediment, a style of dormer new to the town of New Castle. The side facing Third Street features quarter-round windows on the third level. Van Dyke died soon after the house was built, and it passed to his son, Kensey Johns Van Dyke, and it is by that name that the house is known.

All of the four houses just described are town houses, that is, a residence in an urban setting. They are all detached and unusually large and stylish, as befit the level of wealth and social position of their owners. Yet even though those houses were high-end, they were in no way trendsetting or flashy. They bespoke a preference for a type of conservative design and construction appropriate for a second-tier town—a town long a political and legal center but not one with a level of wealth or need for grand-scale buildings, public or private, that would stand in the forefront of

Front door of the Kensey Johns Van Dyke House.

modern architectural design, as Benjamin Henry Latrobe acerbically noted in his journal in 1806.

New Castle did not set architectural trends; it followed them as it became a town of townhouses. Most of the houses of Federal New Castle, however, were not as grand nor as ornately decorated as the previous examples. Most fell into the categories of adjoining or attached structures, duplexes or row houses. In modern parlance, they might be called townhouses. Rows of contiguous houses date back in Europe for centuries. The beauty of the Georgian-Federal townhouse as it developed first in England and then in America was its shape, which could be expanded or contracted to fit lot sizes and the needs of owners and developers. Just as townhouses were easily adapted by size, so too could they be adapted in their level of exterior ornamentation. Townhouses could be large detached buildings, or they could be built in multiples. They might actually be separate houses that abutted each other to form a row look, or they could share common walls and be built to a common pattern inside and out.

By the early nineteenth century New Castle contained a number of abutting or joined townhouses ranging in size and level of architectural detailing. Three examples demonstrate the types of attached housing available to people of various levels of income in early-nineteenth-century New Castle.

The Archibald Alexander Houses

Archibald Alexander, wealthy physician and town leader, built the three-story brick double house at 26 and 28 Third Street circa 1800 in the Federal style. The placement of the entry doors and their combined surround emphasized the joined nature of the structure. This high-style surround features pilasters and crown with punch-and-gouge work. The finely carved keystones above the

Archibald Alexander Houses, 26 and 28 East Third Street. From the Latrobe Survey. *(Courtesy of Delaware Public Archives)*

windows on the first-floor of Number 26 are particularly noteworthy. At first glance the two sides of the building appear to be mirror images, but if you look carefully you will note that the house on the left, Number 26, is a bit narrower than Number 28. Number 26 also has a dormer, but that is a later addition. Slight differences aside, the height and width of the building make it a commanding presence as it faces the Green. If Dr. Alexander wanted to make an architectural statement, he did. If he wanted to earn income, he did that too,

26 and 28 East Third Street today.

for he lived on one side and rented the other.

Aull's Row Three two-and-a-half-story frame houses, collectively known as Aull's Row, stand at 47, 49, and 51 Second Street and date to 1802. Today they display no uniformity of facades, but they were built as a single unit with one ridgepole running the length of the row. Interestingly, one unit, Number 47, is wider than the other two. John Aull was a carpenter who immigrated to New Castle from Ireland with his brother, William, a merchant, in about 1800. He built a number of other houses on The Strand and on Second Street and died in 1828 a wealthy man.

Aull built this row along what would then have been the stable side of houses facing the river, such as the adjacent George Read, Jr., property. His choice of construction material marks the houses as intended for less affluent tenants than those who inhabited the larger, higher-style houses. Aull's Row is a rare example of what might be called a vernacular

Aull's Row, 47-51 East Second Street.

style of simple, unadorned wooden boxes. Amazingly they have survived fire since the first years of the nineteenth century.

Cloud's Row A larger row, today numbered 17-23 Delaware Street and 1 East Second Street, was built about 1804. The row consisted of seven dwellings, each three-and-a-half stories tall and one room deep.

Cloud's Row, 17-23 Delaware Street and 1 East Second Street. From the Latrobe Survey. *(Courtesy of Delaware Public Archives)*

The developer, Harlan Cloud, descended from an early Quaker family. He lived in Chester County, Pennsylvania, and Wilmington, Delaware, but appears never to have lived in New Castle. Cloud's Row was purely a speculative venture, perhaps influenced by similar large-scale projects recently undertaken in Philadelphia to build rows of identical houses. Even though Harlan Cloud built for profit rather than as a personal statement, the facades of Cloud's Row exhibit several pleasing Federal style design elements such as stone door and window lintels and a continuous stone beltcourse that provide a sense of unity and style to these small dwellings. The facades on the first floor have changed many times, but their restoration in the mid-twentieth century has returned

Photograph, ca. 1949, of Cloud's Row taken for Perry, Shaw and Hepburn survey. *(Courtesy of New Castle Historical Society)*

them to the appearance of their era of construction. If you look up to the untouched upper floors, you can count seven dormers, although one doorway has been bricked in.

CHANGING TECHNOLOGIES, CHANGING PRODUCTS FOR BUILDING NEW CASTLE

Until the early nineteenth century human hands produced virtually all building materials. This era of craft production limited both the range and the quantity of products available. Then in about 1820 came the commercial application of waterpower and new machinery to assist in fashioning a wide range of building materials. Water-powered mills could produce millions of feet of lumber and the nails needed to hold a house together, which in turn led to balloon-frame houses, so much faster and easier to build than the old timber-framed structures. Machines could make bricks, dress stone, and turn out cast- and wrought-iron. Glass production improved, and by the 1850s large sheets of plate glass could be used in store windows. Changing products also allowed for changes in rooflines, as new waterproof composition materials made flatter roofs possible.

By the 1830s steam began to replace water as the major source of industrial power, which led to the creation of new machines and processes that could use that new power. Once again levels of production and range of products leaped forward. Band saws replaced circular saws in churning out lumber, and scroll and jig saws produced a wide range of standardized, relatively inexpensive yet ornate, wooden ornamentation for the exteriors and interiors of houses. The quality and quantity of pressed brick and terra cotta increased as did new mortar products. The range of paint colors also increased. Those products were used, inside and out, to create buildings full of exuberant "gingerbread" styling that mixed and matched materials and colors, making possible the creation of buildings often termed "Victorian."

Moving Beyond the Georgian-Federal in the Nineteenth Century

New Castle is best known for its Georgian and Federal buildings, styles that emphasized regularity and restraint and that remained popular in the town for over one hundred years. New Castle was slow to change, even though new styles were appearing throughout America by the 1830s. In part the reason was that the town was not growing, so the buildings of the past continued to serve. In 1837 there was a depression in the economy of the United States that preceded rapid industrialization and the spread of steam-powered railroads and ships. That same year the eighteen-year-old Princess Victoria became Queen of England. Her long reign would see an international movement in architecture toward exuberance and eclecticism that we now call "Victorian." The styles that we associate with the mid-to-late nineteenth century include most notably those known as Greek Revival, Italianate, Gothic Revival,

Second Empire and Queen Anne. New Castle offers excellent examples of each of those Victorian-era styles.

Industrialization, railroads, and steamships changed New Castle as they changed the rest of the world. With those changes came renewed growth. As New Castle began to grow, new styles came to the old town. Those styles—and their adaptations over time—range from a few high-style examples to more vernacular examples and are well worth seeing. Had the Historic New Castle plan laid out by Perry, Shaw and Hepburn in the 1940s been implemented there would be far fewer of them left to show.

Greek Revival Style

The small number of extant houses built in New Castle in those depression years of the late 1830s and 1840s can be loosely categorized as Greek Revival architecture. Between 1830 and 1860 it was the dominant style of architecture in America, ubiquitous from the New England farmhouse to the southern plantation house, from eastern urban mansions and townhouses to the houses constructed by settlers moving ever-westward. What made the style so popular was its adaptability. Architects could design high-style buildings with elaborate columned porches, porticos, and moldings, but skilled local builders could also borrow from pattern books to create vernacular adaptations of what was essentially the old tried-and-true box-like building. All of the Greek Revival buildings in New Castle fall into the category of vernacular architecture.

In New Castle, the best way to tell the difference between a Greek Revival structure and those built earlier is to look at the roofline. The new style displayed a lower pitch than earlier styles, which in turn allowed for the creation of a full third floor rather than dormer windows in attic space. The facades of all of the Greek Revival buildings in town are extremely plain, from their simple brick corbelled cornices to the plain white window sills and lintels made of stone or wood. As in earlier styles, front doors remain an architectural focus. Those doors can be flush or slightly recessed, surrounded by simple framing, usually but not always, topped by a rectangular transom. Gone are the Federal-style fanlights and richly carved surrounds. Some but not all doors and transoms are "crowned" by heavy entablatures in vaguely classical styles.

The doorways of 117 and 119 East Third Street include transoms above the doors and a shared dentiliated entablature held up by pilasters in the classical Ionic style.

All of the buildings in New Castle that can be categorized as Greek Revival, at least in spirit, are two- and three-bay-wide houses. The closest approximation to a Greek design can be seen in the ionic pilasters on the doorways of 117 and 119 East Third Street, built about 1840. Those doors are positioned together and share an entablature.

A row of four houses, numbers 10-16 East Fourth Street, also date to about 1840. These narrow two-bay-wide houses, like many Greek Revival houses, have smaller windows on the third floor than on the floors below. The facades of these houses clearly reject the formal symmetry of window and door alignment so important in earlier styles.

Other examples of the Greek Revival style from the 1840s and 1850s can be seen scattered throughout New

10 and 12 East Fourth Street are half of a row of houses built about 1840 in a vernacular Greek Revival style.

30 and 32 West Fourth Street exemplify the vernacular Greek Revival style.

Castle, particularly on the east side of town, but there is a good row of four at numbers 26, 28, 30, and 32 West Fourth Street. Indeed, many of the houses built for the town's growing working class well into the late nineteenth century continued to contain hints of the vernacular Greek Revival style.

Italianate Style

Victorian-era architectural styles look not only to the ancient worlds of Greece and Rome, but also to medieval forms adapted from all parts of Europe. Not only do buildings manifest different looks, they also project different sensibilities on a continuum from rational to nostalgic. Just as the search for intelligent illumination of the Enlightenment gave way to the Romantic in philosophy and literature, so did it in the arts, including architecture. The Italianate marks a transition from the ancient to the romantic.

Tuscany provided the inspiration for the Italianate style. As they introduced new styles, new shapes, new materials, and new ornamentation into America, some architects looked to old rural villas for design ideas, while others borrowed from the urban buildings of Renaissance Florence. Although the most expansive designs of urban palazzos and rustic villas were built in places such as the Hudson River Valley in New York, there are a large number of buildings scattered throughout New Castle that exhibit design elements and details of the Italianate style.

Italianate houses, like Greek Revival ones, generally have roof lines that are low pitched or almost flat, but only Italianate houses have distinctive heavy, bracketed cornices. They are instantly distinguishable from the denticulated or corbelled cornices of classically inspired architecture. Windows and doors, whether rectangular or arched, single or paired, were surrounded by heavy frames that are often arched at the top. Italianate-style windows have only two panes of glass, divided vertically, per sash, and those on the first floor are often taller than those above. Builders in the Italianate style sometimes used brick as had their Georgian and Federal predecessors, but they were also prone to use darker materials, especially brownstone. Yet Italianate houses in New Castle do not break with the past in terms of footprint. They remain box-like, two or three floors high, and built of brick, wood, or, in at least one case, of brownstone.

The Farmers Bank Building The view from the corner of Delaware Street and The Strand includes rows of buildings that reflect the Georgian and Federal eras. But there is one anomaly: the large two-story structure that stands at number 4 The Strand. This dignified building offers an excellent opportunity to introduce the Italianate style and to contrast it to the Federal and Georgian buildings around it. The building has a cubic structure and a low-pitched roof. Its foundation is brownstone, a soft, easily worked stone found in the Connecticut River Valley that became popular first in New York and then in Philadelphia and beyond. The quoined corners are made of rusticated, painted iron, providing a striking contrast to the brick walls and large windows, which are rounded at the top and feature scrolled brackets.

The building is set back from the sidewalk by an elaborate iron fence and small yard on The Strand side. The walls are constructed of a rosy colored brick that further sets the building apart from its neighbors. The rear section was added in the late nineteenth century.

This building has an interesting history. It was built in 1850-51 to be the Farmers Bank, and it continued to serve that function until 1899, when the bank

Photograph of 4 The Strand when it served as the office of the Farmers Bank. The steps on Delaware Street led to the bank entrance, while the door on The Strand led to the bank manager's living quarters. *(Courtesy of New Castle Historical Society)*

4 The Strand today.

consolidated its operations and moved its New Castle assets to Wilmington. The Farmers Bank was chartered by the State of Delaware in 1807 to be both the repository of the state's money and a commercial bank. Branches were to be established in each of the three counties.

New Castle men, including George Read, Jr., and Kensey Johns, helped to establish the bank and served on its board. New Castle's leaders had hoped to have the major branch located in their town, but the leaders of Dover, the state capital, dashed that hope. Still, as a county seat, New Castle got a branch. The bank's first location in New Castle was in a building owned by George Read, Jr., next to his house on The Strand and now part of its garden. In 1817 the bank purchased the house at Number 6 The Strand for its use.

As the bank's business grew, it needed a purpose-built structure. Next door to its then location was a large vacant lot, known as the "burnt lot," where the house of Colonel John French had stood in colonial times. In 1850 the Farmers Bank bought the lot and hired John McArthur, Jr., (1823-1890) a young Philadelphia architect, to build their bank.

McArthur was to have a meteoric career that epitomizes the American Dream. A native of Scotland, he came to Philadelphia at the age of ten to live with his uncle, a master builder. While apprenticed as a house carpenter, young McArthur learned about architectural design by attending lectures at places throughout the city such as the Franklin Institute. He earned his first major commission in 1848

A sensitive alteration transformed the bank's doorway into a window with a low balcony at the time the whole building became a private residence.

to build the Philadelphia House of Refuge. The Farmers Bank hired him soon thereafter. McArthur went on to have a spectacularly successful career building hotels, offices, houses, and government buildings. Today he is best remembered for his design and construction of the Philadelphia City Hall, a huge project that he began in 1872 but did not live to see completed.

In the 1850s the Italianate style was very much in vogue. The style suggested the Renaissance and, in the case of a bank, recalled the Medici bankers of Florence. The building at 4 The Strand is a restrained example of that style. Even after the Farmers Bank moved out in 1899, another bank, the Wilmington and Brandywine, located its office there until 1904.

Number 4 The Strand was built with two entrances: one faced Delaware Street for access to the bank and the other faced The Strand and was the entryway for the cashier and his family who lived above. On the night of September 30, 1887, there was a daring robbery attempt at the bank. The newspaper account of the robbery also gives us a clear picture of how the family used their living quarters on the second floor.

The building you see today has been carefully and respectfully altered to be a single-family residence. The stone stairway that once led to the bank entrance on Delaware Street has been removed and the door replaced by a window surrounded by a small metal railing.

The Farmers Bank was an important institution in New Castle. Its officers made loans to local businessmen and to the Trustees of the Common. The bank subscribed to shares in the Gap and Newport Turnpike Company and in the Frenchtown Turnpike and Railroad Company, both very important to New Castle's development.

The Sheriff's House The two-story brownstone building that fronts onto Second Street on the Green behind the courthouse offers another example of the Italianate style. It was built in 1857-58 to be the home of the New Castle County sheriff, who had charge over the prison that lay both behind and beside the house. The sheriff's house seems unusual among the surrounding red brick Georgian and Federal structures that have survived. That impression would have been different for the century from the 1850s to the 1950s, when the Presbyterian Gothic-style church of brownstone stood just across

THE MORNING NEWS
Wilmington, Del., Saturday, October 1, 1887
BURGLARS FOILED
MASKED MEN FAIL TO ROB NEW CASTLE'S BANK
Cashier Cooper Shoots a Villain in the Face—A series of Thrilling Events.

Newspaper readers throughout Delaware learned what the people of New Castle were already discussing on every street corner. The robbers had come to the bank, well equipped with a ladder, chisels, blasting powder, and a wheelbarrow to carry away the loot they hoped to extract from the bank vault. They placed the ladder under an open window on the second story on the northeast side of the building facing The Strand. Three masked men climbed up and entered a room occupied by Cashier Richard G. Cooper's visiting brother-in-law, a United States diplomat. Two of the robbers bound him and nearly smothered him with bedclothes, while the third entered the central hallway and knocked on the door of the next bedroom, which was occupied by Cooper's daughter. Hearing the noise down the hall, Cashier Cooper took a revolver from his bureau. Opening his bedroom door, he was confronted by the masked robber, who was carrying a gun and a lantern. Not seeing Cooper's weapon, the robber ordered the cashier, "Don't say a word." Cooper did not. Instead he fired his revolver directly into the robber's face. The startled robber also fired, but he missed. Meanwhile, one of the robbers in the brother-in-law's room panicked. "The game's up!," he shouted. All three then descended the ladder, the wounded man leaving pools of blood everywhere. They ran across the railroad track toward the Battery and apparently escaped by boat, leaving their equipment behind.

the street. If the sheriff's house seems a bit grim, it is worth recalling that it was placed adjacent to a prison, whipping post, pillory, and place of execution, now all gone.

The sheriff's house is a dignified, symmetrical structure that features a projecting center to add interest to its five-bay-wide front. The building's Italianate features include windows with rounded, or arched, tops and a matching front door, and quoined corners. Only

Sheriff's House in the 1940s when it was the New Castle Club. *(Courtesy of New Castle Historical Society)*

the triangular pediment, with a cornice that features large modillions, suggests any nod to the buildings in its vicinity. A careful look at the malleable brownstone surfaces will reveal four levels of stone dressing. The smoothest, most fully dressed stones were used in the belt courses and window and door surrounds. The front walls are slightly less smooth, while the foundations are rough-cut blocks with smoothed edges. Least fashioned of all are the stones used to build the walls of the prison sections on the sides and in the rear of the house.

Examples of levels of dressing, or finishing, of the brownstone used to build the Sheriff's House.

Brownstone was used here and in such a precise way because of the requirements of Samuel Sloan, the rising young Philadelphia architect who was responsible for the building's design. Samuel Sloan (1815-1884) was noted for his construction of numerous hospitals as well as for his elaborate Italianate villas designed for wealthy clients. His first big commission was for the Delaware County Courthouse in Media, Pennsylvania, in 1849. That building no doubt caught the attention of New Castle County's leaders when they sought to construct a home for their sheriff and a new prison a few years later.

The sheriff's house has restrained decorative features that differentiated it from the more severe prison that Sloan designed to be built behind it. With the construction of the workhouse at Greenbank, Delaware, in 1899, the prison was no longer needed and most of

View of the Sheriff's House and adjoining prison entrance that was removed about 1900. *(Courtesy of New Castle Historical Society)*

THE RAID THAT CAUGHT THE NEW CASTLE CLUB BY SURPRISE

Beginning in the 1930s, the Sheriff's House on the Green, became the home of the New Castle Club, a popular place for many of the town's leading men. At least part of the club's popularity rested upon access to its ten illegal slot machines. The location of the machines was common knowledge, so periodically the police raided the club. With one exception, they always came up short because tip-offs allowed members to hide the slots in advance of a raid. Unfortunately, in 1958, according to town legend, the member forewarned of the raid had too much to drink and forgot to tell his fellow members. State troopers, city police, and an inspector of the Alcoholic Beverage Control Commission carried out the raid and confiscated the slots.

Since the club's membership included many of the town's leaders, a number of businessmen, lawyers, and politicians felt great unease after the raid. Embarrassment loomed. In the end, though, only the club steward and another employee were fined. The membership escaped censure, but slot machines never returned to the New Castle Club. Without the slots, enthusiasm for the club declined, and it eventually closed in the late 1960s, ending the most popular, and memorable, use of the old Sheriff's House.

it was torn down. The house remained and has had various uses, including a brief stint as a hospital ward during the Spanish Flu epidemic of 1918 and as a private club complete with "one-armed bandits." Eventually it reassumed its law-and-order role by becoming the town's police station. More recently it has been a part of the state-supported Courthouse Museum and is to be the Delaware headquarters of the United States Park Service.

The creators of the house and prison demonstrated pride in their accomplishment by erecting a stone plaque that can still be seen on the northeast side of the building facing onto the Green. The plaque gives the name of architect Samuel Sloan along with the names of the building contractors and the building committee.

Saint Peter the Apostle Roman Catholic Church New Castle has one other major building designed in Italianate style. It is Saint Peter the Apostle Roman Catholic Church, located a few blocks northwest from the Green at Fifth and Harmony streets. The church is in the midst of a largely working-class residential district that recalls New Castle's industrial development in the late nineteenth century and the faith of the Irish and later the Italian immigrants who worshipped there. Many of them and their descendants lie buried in the cemetery adjacent to the church.

There were a few Catholics in New Castle as early as 1766, but not un-til 1806 were they numerous enough to purchase the lot on which Saint Peter's now stands. The first church building there was a wooden cha-pel, which was later replaced by a small brick church that served the communi-ty for sixty-plus years. By 1870 the num-ber of Catholics had

Bell tower, church, and rectory of Saint Peter's the Apostle par-ish were built between 1876 and 1896. This open view would be impossible to get today because of automobiles, poles, and wires. *(Courtesy of New Castle Historical Society)*

outgrown their small church, and the present building was constructed and consecrated in 1876. The rectory followed in 1877, and the campanile, or bell tower, was added in the 1890s. The tower was built as a memorial to parishioner John Brady by his family, immigrants from Ireland who had first worked in the Triton Textile Mill and then advanced to own a grocery and cigar store near their home by the railway station at Ninth and Young streets.

In the early twentieth century a large brick entryway with a sweeping double staircase replaced the two original staircases that had started at ground level on both sides of the building and led up to the front doorway at the second level. Interior alterations over

Saint Peter's Italianate style bell tower.

time generally reflected changing stylistic tastes, but the opening of the altar area after the mandated liturgical changes of the 1960s brought a more open and restrained look to the sanctuary.

Although Saint Peter's was built at a time when the congregation and pastorate were mainly Irish, the building and its bell tower are based on Italian models. Perhaps the view was that if the Protestants were building Gothic structures, the Catholics would emphasize the older traditions of church architecture from the region around Rome. Whatever the reasons for the choice, the church must have been a welcome sight to the Italian immigrants who began coming to New Castle around 1900.

The church building is a simple rectangular structure with gable end facing the street. It features rounded, or arched, windows and overhanging eaves supported by scrolled brackets on a deep wooden panel with rectangular moldings between brackets. That roof-level rhythm is carried through the walls in the brickwork that features both vertical and horizontal patterns. The most prominent Italian-inspired feature is the tall, square campanile capped by a belfry and a cross. Seeing it is almost like being in an Italian town. By contrast, the rectory on the opposite side of the church, with its gabled roof and mostly rectangular windows, is similar to the composite architecture of houses that were being constructed for middle-class buyers elsewhere in New Castle in the 1870s.

35 West Fifth Street A good example of a typical modest Italianate townhouse stands at 35 West Fifth Street. Its roof is low-pitched, and the cornice boasts three pairs of heavy brackets set within a deep and fancily molded panel that hold up the projecting eave. On the façade, lightly recessed rectangular-shaped double doors and an oval-shaped light are surrounded by a curving wood frame arched at the top and surmounted by a slightly raised hood of lighter colored brick. Brick hoods also top the arched windows, each divided vertically into two panes per sash. The side windows in the main block and rear extension, or ell, have no hoods. Perhaps harkening back to the idea of an Italian piazza, a porch runs the full length of the ell and exhibits columns topped by ornamental scrollwork and set upon a spindled railing.

35 West Fifth Street. A heavy, bracketed cornice with a molded panel disguises the flatness of the roofline.

35 West Fifth Street, a vernacular Italianate house, boasts many fine decorative details.

The house at 35 West Fifth Street is also an excellent example of the area's development process. By the time of the Civil War an industrial building covered much of the block. Then industrialist Thomas Tasker began to acquire land there. Between 1876 and 1883 the holder of the deed to the land at 35 West Fifth changed hands eight times before the splendid vernacular Italianate townhouse was built.

227 Chestnut Street By appearance alone, 227 Chestnut Street might seem a strange choice for inclusion as an examplar of an architectural style, but in its original form, it was unique for New Castle. Here was a plain Italianate-style house with connecting service wing, carriage house, and stable, the perfect arrangement for the harsh winter weather of New England. Ira Lunt built the complex when he moved his family from Maine to New Castle in the 1870s. Lunt served in the Civil War and worked as a stone mason in Maine. He came to New Castle to build ice-breaking piers in the harbor.

The house itself is a simple two-bay-wide, two-story-tall box with a flat roof. A wide, plain cornice with pairs of machine-turned brackets holds up the roof's overhanging eaves. A double door with arched glass panels supplies the only ornamentation to the frame structure, except perhaps for the German-style drop siding, where each horizontal board displays a concave edge at its top. The service ell at the

New England style house in Delaware, 227 Chestnut Street.

Detail of doorway,
227 Chestnut Street.

rear of the house has a full-length porch marked by columns and simple scroll-worked decorations. Unfortunately, other sections of the complex are now gone, so one can no longer appreciate the structure's original expansiveness.

The Gothic Revival

The Gothic Revival co-existed with the Italianate and with other more classically based approaches to architecture. It is generally easy to identify because Gothic buildings are designed to evoke the Middle Ages. They recall a romantic view of medieval times such as one would find in the novels of Sir Walter Scott. The style was widely used to build churches and colleges and could be adapted to construct houses from cottages to mansions. Its hallmark features included tall, narrow windows, some with stained glass, and arched or pointed tops. There are also asymmetrical floor plans that feature projecting alcoves and towers, and steeply pitched gabled roofs, often with finial-topped crossed gables from which hung intricately decorated bargeboards.

The Lesley Mansion Visitors to New Castle may be surprised to discover that the town offers a remarkable building that demonstrates all of the major Gothic Revival characteristics and is one of the best examples of a Gothic

Revival house to be found anywhere in Delaware. It is the Lesley Mansion, located on a large lot in the southwest part of the town between Sixth and Seventh streets and Tremont and South streets.

The Lesley Mansion, New Castle's finest Gothic Revival house.

Allen Voorhees Lesley, a medical doctor, was a native of Philadelphia and an honors graduate of the University of Pennsylvania. His father, a cabinet-maker by trade, was hired by the Chesapeake and Delaware Canal Company to be its secretary-treasurer. It was through that connection that the doctor-to-be lived for a time as a young man on a farm near Delaware City and came to know New Castle. He married in 1844 and moved to live in the town, where his convivial nature, learning, and professional skill earned him many friends and financial success.

In 1855 the popular doctor contracted with the architects Thomas and James M. Dixon to build a Gothic-inspired house on a large suburban lot southwest of New Castle that overlooked the river and offered the opportunity for extensive gardens. The Dixons were well-known architects who had been born in Wilmington but practiced their craft from Baltimore. Thomas Dixon is known especially for his design of the Gothic-inspired Mount Vernon Place Methodist Church in Baltimore and for Wilmington's Second Em-

The front lawn of the Lesley Mansion at its full horticultural glory before portions of the property were sold and developed. *(Courtesy of New Castle Historical Society)*

pire style Grand Opera House, both done in the 1870s.

The thirty-five-room Lesley Mansion encapsulates nearly all of the features associated with the Gothic Revival style. Its square tower with a pointed roof featuring small recessed triangular windows can be seen from blocks away. A view of the house from a nearby street illustrates the exterior details of highly ornate bargeboards, particularly over the tall gables of the roofline and the projecting front doorway; a beveled water table; and windows of various sizes and shapes, all with cast-iron sills. This is a private home, so sightseers cannot get too close, but the magnificence of the builder's intention can be easily grasped from afar. The extensive gardens, filled with exotic, imported plantings so favored in Victorian times, once filled the entire block. They have now been scaled back as the edges of the property were sold and row houses erected, but some large trees and the carriage house are still visible.

Dr. Lesley and his wife loved their home and entertained townspeople regularly. They also traveled the world, where he sketched scenes of local life. The doctor served terms as a state senator and was an active Mason. When Mrs. Lesley died, Dr. Lesley was disconsolate. He ceased entertaining and sought relief in foreign travel. He died in 1881 at age 59, but his house and artwork, some now in museums and private collections, live on.

The next important resident of the mansion was Selden Scranton Deemer, the steel manufacturer, house builder, and creator of Deemer's Beach Amusement Park. Deemer was noted for his charitable works in New Castle. Most especially, he gave an annual Christmas party for the children of poor families. When the Depression struck, he discontinued the parties and instead provided food, clothing, and fuel for many of New Castle's poor. His death in 1934 was a blow to the whole town.

22 and 24 West Fourth Street Numbers 22 and 24 West Fourth Street are a perfect example of a double house built in the Gothic Revival style. Acquila Hizar bought the land in 1876 and shortly thereafter work began on his house, which was Number 24. Hizar, a bricklayer and contractor, played a large role in the construction process, but he chose to create for himself and his wife an architect-designed house. His architect of choice was Isaac Harding Hobbs and Son of Philadelphia. As a practical businessman, Hizar added a mirror image of his house, at Number 22, as a rental unit.

Isaac H. Hobbs, Jr., followed a traditional mid-nineteenth-century path from carpenter to architect. An undeniable self-promoter, Hobbs gained national fame through plans published for twenty years in *Godey's Ladies Book*, probably the most widely read monthly magazine in America, particularly designed for the rising middle class, and then in two editions of his book *Hobbs'*

Architecture (1873,1876). Hobbs and his son George also offered a mail-order service for house plans. The firm designed some churches, schools, and commercial buildings, but concentrated on houses. Their work can best be characterized as mid- to late-nineteenth-century eclectic, a quintessential American High Victorian expression drawing upon elements from Gothic Revival through Queen Anne styles. At its best it provided clients with houses whose exteriors mixed colors, materials, and elevations and whose

Late-nineteenth-century photograph of Mr. and Mrs. Acquila Hizar. *(Courtesy of New Castle Historical Society)*

22-24 West Fourth Street, double house built by Acquila Hizar.

interiors emphasized rooms with high ceilings, substantial woodwork, and levels of detailing sought by the middle class.

The plan provided for Captain Hizar, a Civil War rank he used throughout the rest of his life, shares some features with one shown in Hobbs' plan book of 1876, but Hizar's house is less fussy and projects a greater robustness in presentation. Plans for the Hizar house at Number 24 still exist, and they show that changes were made during construction. The final product is a tall, three-story brick structure that embraces irregularity of shape and late-nineteenth-century decoration. It features a steep, cross-gabled roof with exposed rafter ends, corbelled brick chimney, and wrought-iron tracery. Arched bargeboards with elaborate cutwork and scalloped cross bracing fill the gable end to the top of the third-floor window, adding character and asserting dramatic verticality. The projecting wood bay window of the sitting room is topped by a flat roof that runs across the deeply recessed entryway to create a porch with its own elaborate bracketing.

Second Empire

The term "Second Empire" is given to an eclectic, exuberant style that became popular in the United States during the prosper-

Detail of Number 24 showing the decorative woodwork of the front gable.

ous years that followed the Civil War. As an historic period, the "Second Empire" denotes the reign of Napoleon III, the Emperor of the French from 1851 to 1871. The emperor encouraged opulence in everything. The style of the era is marked most especially by the splendor of the Paris Opera Garnier, built in the 1860s, and by the broad avenues of Paris that display rows of uniform yet ornate buildings topped by mansard roofs.

Americans used the Second Empire style to construct large public buildings and grand halls, as well as houses. The style's major characteristics include the use of multiple colors and materials set in elaborate, yet symmetrical patterns. With the exception of the roof, it is a style that often looks like the Italianate gone to extremes. Second Empire buildings, especially houses, usually include the use of roofs that are almost vertical and shingled. These are called "mansard" roofs to recall the name of a seventeenth-century French architect. Other characteristics of the style include tall, arch-topped windows, heavy moldings, and ornamented porches.

New Castle may seem an unusual place to find Second Empire buildings, yet the town does contain a number of examples in that style.

The Masonic Hall / Opera House If you walk up from the river along Delaware Street soaking in the colonial and Federal atmosphere around you, a large, proudly imposing structure that clearly comes from another time confronts you and demands a second look. Glancing upward you will see a plaque attached to the middle of the top floor that displays symbols of the Masonic Order and the Odd Fellows and proclaims that the building was "Erected in 1879." This is the Masonic Hall and Opera House, and it represents New Castle's best example of the Second Empire style.

The Opera House was constructed at a discouraging time in New Castle. The state legislature had just enacted a law to build a modern New Castle County Courthouse in Wilmington. For the first time in its history New Castle would no longer be a county seat. Many of the town's leading men were lawyers. How many of them would remain in town? In the face of this potentially serious blow, it took courage and optimism for the Masons and Odd Fellows to agree to vacate their meeting space on the top floor of the Town Hall and to build an opera house with lodge meeting rooms. The

The Second-Empire style Masonic Hall and Opera House is a commanding presence along Delaware Street. *(Courtesy of New Castle Historical Society)*

lodges appointed a joint committee to undertake the work. The leader was William Herbert, one of New Castle's most active citizens, a businessman and politician who served in many county and state offices, including county sheriff and state treasurer. William Herbert was a booster determined to restore New Castle's damaged civic pride.

The man chosen to design the opera house was Theophilus P. Chandler, Jr. (1845-1928). Chandler was one of Philadelphia's most professionally accomplished architects. The founder of the Depart-

Early view of Masonic Hall and Opera House, built 1879. This is another of the buildings that were slated for demolition by the Perry, Shaw and Hepburn plan of the late 1940s. *(Courtesy of New Castle Historical Society)*

ment of Architecture at the University of Pennsylvania, he designed all manner of buildings including churches, commercial structures, and residences. He was the favorite architect of the du Pont family for whom he made a number of residential designs, including an addition to Winterthur.

During the year that Chandler worked on the New Castle Opera House he was simultaneously constructing the new courthouse in Wilmington, which was also in the style of the Second Empire. The courthouse in Wilmington lasted for only a generation and was razed at the end of World War I to make way for Rodney Square, but the New Castle Opera House still stands. Only an accomplished professional could have designed such a large structure, measuring 50 feet by 100 feet at its base and standing three stories high. The tallest floor is the second, which housed a hall with a stage and seating capacity for 600 people. This grand room was capable of hosting meetings or traveling shows. The

GRAND OPENING OF NEW CASTLE'S NEW HALL
Ceremonies of Dedication
Immense Display—Good Music
September 13, 1880

"This is a big day for New Castle, and celebrates a plucky and hopeful step in the town's new departure," said a Wilmington newspaper. A crowd estimated at between 10,000 and 15,000 people, the largest gathering in New Castle's history, assembled to witness the dedication of the splendid new Opera House. The three-story building will serve two principal fraternal organizations: the St. John's Lodge of Ancient Free and Accepted Masons and the Washington Lodge of Odd Fellows. To celebrate this event large contingents of lodge members in full parade regalia came by steamboat and railway from Philadelphia, Wilmington, and Salem and Camden, New Jersey, and other towns in the region. As bands played and steamboat whistles blew, the lodge members marched up Delaware Street from the wharf to the "imposing and ornamental Hall."

Long tables laid out with sandwiches, pies, cakes, and fruit greeted visitors at the dock, next to the Town Hall, and in the public square. Buildings along all the major streets were "profusely and gorgeously decorated with flags and flowers." The Opera House itself was festooned with signal flags lent for the occasion by the revenue cutter *USS Hamilton,* which was in the harbor. The day climaxed with the Rev. J.H. Caldwell's sermon describing Biblical analogies such as the dedication of Solomon's Temple. In the evening there was a grand ball led by William Herbert, the man most responsible for seeing the project through. Dancing continued until dawn.

The Wilmington press noted the special significance of the new building as a forward step for a town that was losing the county seat. For too long, according to one newsman, New Castle residents had relied on giving entertainments in the courthouse. Another writer contrasted the crowds that gathered for the celebration with the "vulgar curiosity" of the somewhat smaller crowds that had long met in New Castle to witness hangings and whippings. "New Castle has reason to be proud of her hall and of the exercises of yesterday. The day will long be noted in her annals as among the greatest she has known." The hall, he predicted, would stand as a symbol of New Castle's growing "spirit of enterprise and energy."

Opera House today, without the cupola, which was removed in 1950.

first floor contained retail shops, and the third floor provided meeting rooms for the Masons and the Odd Fellows.

The New Castle Opera House may not have rivaled the grandeur of the Paris Opera, but for a small American town it had lots of bells and whistles. It is built of brick decorated with rusticated flat stone pilasters and includes a projecting central pavilion, galvanized iron cornice, and quoined corners. There are sets of tall double-arched windows with semi-dressed stone block surrounds featuring keystone centers and caps at the bottoms. The roof edges are enhanced by fence-like balustrades. Four elaborate brick chimneys protrude from the hipped roof. Originally there was also a cupola on the center of the roof at the front of the building. It was removed as a safety hazard in 1950.

The building cost over $30,000, a large sum in 1880. When it proved too costly for the Masons and Odd Fellows to pay the mortgage, William Herbert assumed the debt personally. No wonder New Castle historian Alexander B. Cooper called him "the father of the building," and went on to say that "it stands today largely as a monument to his memory."

125 East Third Street New Castle has a number of houses built in the late nineteenth century that exhibit characteristics of Second Empire style. One of the most elaborately expressive is the house at 125 East Third Street, which records show was built sometime between 1880 and 1888 for William Holschumaker, who got his start in the town as a baker and later became a real-estate speculator.

The house is large with a three-bay-wide front, two-story projection on the side, and high ceilings on the first floor. The back extension with its side porch has lower ceilings. It features an elaborately designed concave-shaped mansard roof, with top and bottom molded cornices, which provides a full third story of living space. For the main block of the house heavy scrolled brackets in pairs of equal size or large and small pairings hold up the roof's projecting overhang and are set on a wide panel ornamented by layers of decorative designs. Brackets and panels on the rear extension are plain. The windows, including those on the first and second floors as well as the richly paneled double front door, are set in arched frames. The windows are decorated with

125 East Third Street, built by William Holschumaker in the 1880s. *(Courtesy of New Castle Historical Society)*

large, artistically carved stone caps and keystones that contrast with the brick surface. A nineteenth-century iron fence encloses the side yard.

Queen Anne Style

Readers of this book may recall the mention of Queen Anne, who ruled in England from 1701 to 1714, in the context of the creation of the battery that was built along the riverfront during Queen Anne's War in 1706. Do not be confused. The architectural style developed in the late nineteenth century and

Detail of 125 East Third Street showing carved stoned caps and keystone used to accent each window.

labeled "Queen Anne" had nothing to do with buildings constructed during her reign. In the late nineteenth century the name sounded quaint, slightly exotic, and definitely pre-Georgian—a perfect appellation for an architectural style.

The Queen Anne style emerged in the 1870s and had run its course by 1900. It was primarily used in the construction of houses. The style was characterized by the use of many contrasting materials, especially slate in geometric designs, and by the urge to go well beyond the restraints of traditional symmetrical, rectangular construction to include turrets, wings, oriel windows, gables, and, especially, ornamented porches. Queen Anne was the last popular style of the exuberantly, "more is better" spirit associated with the Victorian age in America.

101 East Third Street A good example of Queen Anne style in New Castle can be seen at 101 East Third Street. The house stands at the northeast corner of Third at Harmony and was built in 1886-87 to be the parsonage, or rectory, of Immanuel Church. Its architect was W.R. Farrell of Wilmington, and the builder was a local carpenter and contractor, Gardener L. Jemison. According to materials still kept by the church, the vestrymen entertained a number of bids before selecting Jemison, who said he could fulfill the work for the price of $5,600. Jemison's bid was based on the assumption that he could use some inexpensive materials, such as American-made bronze.

The large corner lot on which the house stands gave free reign to the architect, and affords an opportunity to get a sense of the building's stylistic features. As Queen Anne houses go, this is a restrained example, but it does illustrate some significant features of the style. The building defies symmetry. A two-and-a-half story, cross-gable house with gable dormers, it has multiple gabled rooflines to cover its protruding sec-

101 East Third Street.

tions. It is the Queen Anne style's freedom from the restraints of more formal architecture that allows for such a variety of room shapes, all of them well-lit by natural light.

Gable detail, 101 East Third Street.

One has to look closely to discover where the front door is located within the porch with its ornamental wood pillars that wraps around two sides of the building. The brick work includes considerable detailing at the roofline, the chimneys, over the windows, and along the sides. There is also a round window. Geometrically cut slate shingles, a popular feature in Queen Anne houses, are used instead of brick under the roof gables.

The house is a private residence and is no longer the Immanuel rectory. Had the Perry, Shaw and Hepburn colonial revival plan of the 1940s been carried out, it and the other houses along Harmony Street from Market to Third Street would have been torn down to create a parking lot for the sightseeing public.

72 and 80 West Fifth Street Here you will find the houses of the Eliason brothers, Louis E. and James T. Eliason, who came from their family's farm in Saint Georges Hundred to become merchants in New Castle. They were very enterprising young men. In 1873-74 they established a dry-goods business on Delaware Street opposite the courthouse. In 1881 they moved their successful business to the first floor of the new Opera House. About that time they added a new business selling lumber, coal, and farm implements from their own store on South Street, built on land they purchased from Dr. A. V. Lesley. Later yet, they traded in fishing supplies and grain, buying from wholesalers and selling to New Castle's fishermen and millers.

Fueled by their success, in the 1890s the brothers built large homes in the fashionable Queen Anne style near their lumberyard. The house at 72 West Fifth Street was built in 1894; its neighbor at 80 West Fifth Street was constructed five years later in 1899. Both provide excellent examples

72 West Fifth Street, built by Louis E. Eliason.

of the types of Queen Anne houses then being built in towns all over the United States.

Viewed from the front or sides, the Eliason houses present an asymmetrical appearance, starting with off-center front doors. Each house features two-floor bay projections on two sides as well as horizontal and vertical bands of wood trim. Both also have, for New Castle, large yards, which are surrounded by decorative turn-of-the-century iron fencing. The houses were constructed of several contrasting materials, including brick, clapboard, and fish-scale shingles. Their roof lines are cross gabled.

The windows of both houses are large, allowing the residents to catch the natural light, the breeze, and the view from three sides. In summer the Eliasons could relax on the porches that covered the front and one side of each house.

The houses are not clones of each other, however. The J. T. Eliason house at Number 80, the newer of the two, has a deeper, wrap-around porch, which at one end mirrors the curving bow wall of the house. By contrast, Number 72 has a porch across only half of the front façade, which then wraps around the side into a conser-

80 West Fifth Street, built by James T. Eliason.

vatory. Each house has its own set of distinctive decorative details, large and small, that make it unique, but together they were true showcases for the building materials available at the brothers' lumberyard.

The New Castle Library Building The origin of a private library in New Castle goes back to 1811 in the Federal era when the town's most literate citizens joined together to create a subscription library. By 1866 the library, then in the Academy, was open to anyone willing to pay a modest fee for the privilege. The growth in membership and in volumes of books and periodicals led to the library company's decision in 1890 to acquire a lot and construct a suitable building. The structure that you see on East Third Street is the result.

According to signed architectural drawings, the architect who designed this elegant hexagonal building was William Masters Camac (1852-1918), a wealthy and well-traveled man who practiced architecture for a short time in the Philadelphia firm of Furness and Evans. The building has sophisticated features associated with the work of Frank Furness. For example, it makes use of skylights to admit natural light, a technique that Furness had used in his design of the library at the University of Pennsylvania. The building pays homage to the traditional materials and styles of New Castle's past, while introducing new stylistic elements. For example, it uses brick, but in unusual ways, and adds terra cotta accents; it features arches but in oversized form.

The construction of the New Castle Library by a local builder, Harry Mc Caulley, was kept secret from a curious public by a high fence that surrounded the work site. The removal of the fence in the summer of 1892 revealed a building unlike any other in the town. It combined elements of several styles. The hexagonal shape with its slate-shingled

Library, New Castle, Del.

Image of the Old Library when it was young. *(Courtesy of New Castle Historical Society)*

The Old Library building of 1892 was slated for removal in the Perry, Shaw and Hepburn plan of the late 1940s.

and glass pyramidal roof topped by a decorative weathervane immediately draws one's attention. But so does the doorway with its large fanlight featuring geometrical designs surrounded by a massive arch of sandstone that provides striking contrast to the brick exterior. In addition, the bricks on the building's many sides provide yet another visual display with their rhythmic pattern of indented rectangles.

The interior of the building is equally sophisticated. One enters a single large room with bookcases on all sides. Part of the floor is made of glass to admit light to the basement. A carved dark-wood railing surrounds the walkway along the edges of a second floor where additional books could be stored. Eventually even such a cleverly designed space proved too small for townspeople's needs, and the building on East Third Street was retired from library service. It became a property of the Trustees of the Common in 1955 and has been leased to the New Castle Historical Society since 1982.

Into the Twentieth Century: Revival Styles and Bungalows

At the end of the nineteenth century and into the early twentieth century the search for design ideas led architects and house buyers to look backward in time. Some looked to the great buildings of Europe as they built in revival styles. They drew their inspiration for new interpretations from buildings of such styles as Tudor, Georgian, Renaissance, and Chateau. Another group found their inspiration in the homes of artisans and craftsmen of the past. In

New Castle in the era before World War II those national trends led particularly to Colonial Revival and bungalow styles. This variety of styles coexisted, often on the same street, as, for example, West Sixth Street between Tremont and South streets. Of those styles, the bungalow most captured the American imagination in the early twentieth century and led subsequently to the ubiquitous American suburban ranch house.

Bungalow style grew from a smorgasbord of places from Japanese temples, to Spanish haciendas, to worker's cottages in England, to pioneer cabins in America. With Frank Lloyd Wright's Prairie style and Joseph Stickley's craftsman's style helping to lead the way, the bungalow style spread everywhere, sweeping first California and then the whole nation. Over time, the word *bungalow* came to mean small, one- to one-and-a-half-story detached frame structures that emphasized simple construction techniques. Small size and simplicity of construction meant less expense. Some companies, such as Sears Roebuck, even offered pre-cut models that arrived ready for assembly. One such example can be seen at Fourth and Chestnut streets.

Bungalow did not mean one style but a variety of styles that shared some defining characteristics. Bungalows sit low to the ground and are defined by their roof lines with low pitches and deep eaves. On the exterior, many retain the natural colors of the construction materials, while the interior is arranged for informal living.

108 West Sixth Street　The most distinctive craftsman-style bungalow in New Castle is located at 108 West Sixth Street. It has multiple roof lines, all with gable ends to the street and with long, overhanging roofs and exposed rafters. Its asymmetrical design has a large front porch counterbalanced by a projecting partial second floor. Brackets, half-moon openings on the porch, and shingle siding are just some of the elements of design that characterize both the house and its detached garage. The house and garage are set back from the street by a sturdy, rustic stone wall. Looking at the house head-on, you could imagine it set in a forest clearing, but it sits harmoniously in an urban town in a neighborhood of eclectic styles, including a Dutch Revival house next door and Colonial Revivals across the street.

Craftsman style bungalow at 108 West Sixth Street.

It is a short step in time and place from the west side bungalows of the early twentieth century to the post-World War II suburban developments that now radiate out from the City of New Castle.

THE NEIGHBORHOODS
of NEW CASTLE

The best way to appreciate the interweaving of New Castle's history and architecture is by walking through the town. The final section of this book is designed to enhance your journey.

New Castle is a compact walkable town, and each of its neighborhoods has a distinctive history and character. A walk through time starts in the

Painting by unknown artist entitled "New Castle from Nevins Farm." *(Courtesy of New Castle Historical Society)*

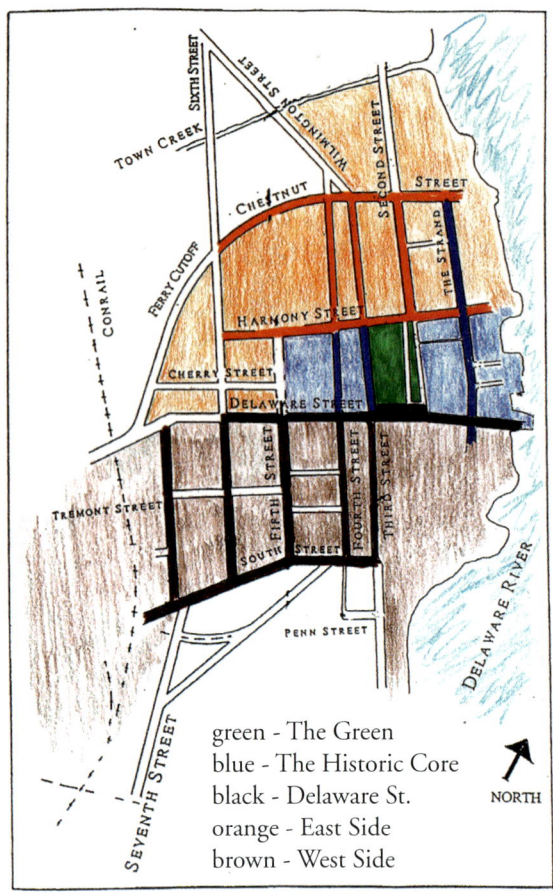

green - The Green
blue - The Historic Core
black - Delaware St.
orange - East Side
brown - West Side

NORTH

historic center, the Green, and then branches out to the old historic core of The Strand through East Fourth Street between Delaware and Harmony streets. That leaves the east side and west side neighborhoods to explore. Geography and history have made Delaware Street the dividing line between the east and west sides of New Castle, which, as you shall see, have distinct characteristics within a shared past.

THE GREEN

The Green has been at the heart of New Castle for most of the town's history. Although it has always been a public space, its uses have evolved to reflect the changing needs of government and of the town's people. It has been a market square, a public square, the seat of state and county governance, and the location of a church. At various times the Green has also shared its park-like space with an arsenal, schools, playgrounds, and a prison that was the site of crowd-drawing lashings and executions. It was also used by some townsmen as a pasture for their animals until that practice was forbidden in 1862. Today the Green is a place for local fairs and is a park where townspeople and visitors can stroll or sit on benches to watch children at play and enjoy the historic architecture that surrounds them.

The Courthouse The building on the Green that is most likely to command a visitor's initial attention is the courthouse. This dominant three-part structure, which flies the flags of the Netherlands, Sweden, and Great Britain

Views from the Green looking east and west.

in addition to the Stars and Stripes, faces a broad section of Delaware Street, where the street was expanded to incorporate part of the original market square. Since 1955 the building and the surrounding Green have been owned and administered by the State of Delaware. The courthouse is now a museum open for tours.

The courthouse has had a complicated history. When William Penn took control of the Three Lower Counties on Delaware from the Duke of York's government in 1682, government was administered from a wooden blockhouse located on the present site of Immanuel Church. It was from that defensive building that Sir Edmund Andros, the duke's representative, held high court in 1675 to hear legal cases, to appoint justices of the peace and tax assessors, to make arrangements for the construction of roads, bridges, and ferries, and to decree regulations for the colonists.

Conviction, altruism, and the desire to encourage settlement led Penn to give his colonists a greater degree of control over their affairs. He was also determined to hold on to the Lower Counties in the face of the claim to the territory by the Calvert family, proprietors of Maryland. In an effort to bind his Province of Pennsylvania to his Three Lower Counties on Delaware, he issued a Frame of Government that created a joint legislature or General Assembly. An equal number of members were to be elected annually by the inhabitants of each county in both colonies. The first meeting of the General Assembly took place in Upland, now Chester, Pennsylvania, in 1682. In 1683 the assembly met in the newly established city of Philadelphia, and in the third year the assembly met in New Castle. Thereafter, meetings always

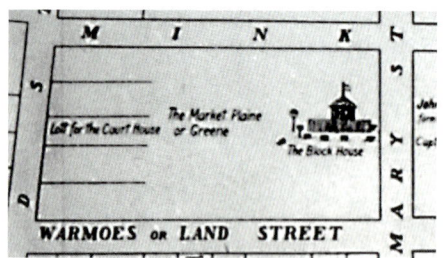

Detail of map by Leon de Valinger showing the Green as ownership of New Castle transferred from the Duke of York to William Penn. *(Courtesy of Delaware Public Archives)*

took place in Philadelphia, except in the years 1690 and 1700, when the assembly met in New Castle because Penn needed to emphasize his proprietorship of the Lower Counties in the face of the Maryland proprietor's lawsuit.

Penn's decision to replace the decayed blockhouse with a county courthouse in New Castle was an important symbol of the Quaker proprietor's shift from the corporate and military governments of the past to a civilian government in which the settlers were participants. Located on a modest hill in the Market Square area facing Delaware Street, a two-story frame courthouse with a cupola was completed circa 1689 on the site of the present courthouse. It served numerous functions. In addition to being New Castle County's seat of justice, it housed the office of the county sheriff, a jail, and, as noted above, on two occasions the General Assembly of Pennsylvania and the Lower Counties met there.

Despite William Penn's best efforts, the residents of the two colonies refused to meld, and Penn was forced to agree to separate assemblies. The first General Assembly of the Lower Counties on Delaware took place in the New Castle Courthouse in 1704. The most dramatic moments in those early years

Courthouse in 1732. Artwork by Peggy Kane. *(Courtesy of Delaware Division of Historical and Cultural Affairs)*

of colonial governance took place in 1715, when a dispute pitted New Castle resident John French, the speaker of the assembly and county sheriff, against Penn's appointed governor. The governor threatened to dissolve the assembly and attempted to arrest Speaker French. Speaker French retreated into the sheriff's office, and the governor's men attacked the door with axes. A riot ensued that drew the assemblymen and most of the town's people to the courthouse in defense of the speaker. When William Penn, by then a sick old man, learned of the dispute, he agreed to replace the high-handed governor.

In 1729 William Kelsey, a convicted thief who was serving time in the courthouse's jail, tried to escape by setting the building on fire. He succeeded in destroying the

Courthouse in 1765 with additions on both sides of central section. Artwork by Peggy Kane. *(Courtesy of Delaware Division of Historical and Cultural Affairs)*

courthouse but was captured and executed for his crime. By that time brick had become the most common building material in the town, and the New Castle County Levy Court, which ran county affairs by levying taxes on its inhabitants, determined to construct a larger and more long-lasting structure. The large central core of the building that you see today, completed in 1732, is the result of their work.

This building has experienced numerous changes, additions, and restorations, yet the present appearance of that original portion is close to what

Courthouse in 1845 after additions and alterations. *(Courtesy of Delaware Division of Historical and Cultural Affairs)*

a colonial passerby would have seen. Then as now, it is a two-story structure with a central doorway and two bays of windows on either side. A balcony overlooks the entryway. There is a balustrade crossing the roof and a cupola in the roof's center. It was from this cupola that the 12-mile circumference that separates Delaware from Pennsylvania was re-calculated in 1752. Anyone with a map and a compass can pinpoint the location of the New Castle Courthouse.

The main differences to the core section's original appearance today are a change in the roofline that followed a fire in 1771 and the re-grading of the street level. The gambrel roof was also discarded in favor of a

Today the Courthouse honors New Castle's evolution from colony to state by flying the flags of the Netherlands, Sweden, United Kingdom, and United States of America. *(Courtesy of Delaware Division of Historical and Cultural Affairs)*

gable style. The street level has been lowered, which necessitated the construction of stairways to the raised, fenced terrace that surrounds the building at the original grade level.

Visitors who take the tour of the courthouse will see the interior as it would have appeared in its most historically significant time, the outbreak of the Revolutionary War. The war took Delaware from being a Penn family proprietorship under English rule to the Delaware State, a part of the United States of America. The courthouse was the meeting place of the Assembly from 1732 until June 1777. It was here that the colonial legislators

The Courthouse today.

protested the Stamp Act and the Townshend Duties; and it was here that, subsequent to a resolution in the Continental Congress meeting in Philadelphia, they voted on June 15, 1776, to separate from Great Britain. The anniversary of that day is now celebrated in New Castle as Separation Day. When you stand on the sidewalk facing the courthouse, you stand where 400 to 500 residents of New Castle County stood on July 24, 1776, to hear the newly adopted national Declaration of Independence read.

Following the decision to separate and to support the creation of a new country, the colonial legislature dissolved itself to permit a convention of elected delegates to write a state constitution. The delegates, led by New Castle resident George Read, Sr., met in the building. Upon completion of their work, the first General Assembly of the State of Delaware met there in October 1776. In May of 1777 the Assembly voted to move the state capital to Dover in Kent County, a more central location and one less vulnerable to the British warships that could sail up the Delaware River.

Day-to-day life in the courthouse was little disturbed by the legislature's departure. The legislators met for only a few weeks of the year, but the work of county government and its courts went on throughout the year. This was, after all, a courthouse, not a state house. Its major function is apparent when you enter the door to see the courtroom that occupies the whole of the space of the main floor. The legislators met upstairs in a room that was usually reserved for grand-jury deliberations. Two smaller buildings were later added to either side

DARING BREAK FROM NEW CASTLE PRISON

Report from the *Delaware Gazette:* On the night of May 2, 1818, four notorious slavenappers staged a daring escape from New Castle's prison on the Green. Three of the four were the Palmer brothers, well-known in the New Jersey-Delaware-Maryland Eastern Shore area as men who captured escaping slaves, or at least African Americans they claimed to be slaves, and sold them in the South. Indicted for slave trading and kidnapping, the men were awaiting trial in New Castle when they broke out—with the help of an outside accomplice.

The unnamed accomplice tied a small auger and saw onto a makeshift rope made of bits of string and other materials that the men had hung out of their second-floor cell window. With those tools, the prisoners then made a hole in the floor through which they dropped down to the main floor using a chain of blankets knotted together. They then crossed the prison yard and began to bore and saw their way through the lower part of the heavy jail door. With the help of their accomplice sawing from the outside, they made an opening large enough to break free. Despite a reward of $200 for their capture, the men vanished back into the shadowy world of slave trading and kidnapping, and the prison suffered an embarrassing breach of security.

of the 1732 structure to house additional court and county functions such as the offices of the register in chancery, clerk of the peace, and recorder of deeds. The building on the east side of the main courthouse was built in two sections: the first in 1765; the second in 1802. The building on the west side dates from 1845. That latter addition, intended to store official records, was to be fireproof, so it is built entirely without wood. These structures continued to serve as the headquarters of New Castle County's court and administration until 1881, when a new courthouse was completed in Wilmington.

There was no jail in the New Castle Courthouse. The Levy Court had learned their lesson from the fire in 1729 and built a separate jail some distance behind the courthouse. That building became a workhouse when another jail was built adjacent to it. This area was the site of executions and floggings that drew crowds of curious onlookers. A few remains of a larger jail built in the 1850s are still visible at the rear of the courthouse, including foundations and two doorways visible high on the rear wall of the sheriff's house. The sheriff's house, a brownstone structure built in 1857-58, is more fully described in the Architecture section.

Immanuel Episcopal Church   The church that stands at the opposite end of the Green from the courthouse is Immanuel Episcopal Church. Its presence in the town square gives an English feel to this American scene. In the reign of Henry VIII the Church of England became the government-supported religion in England. With the coming of English settlers to the area, Anglican worship was introduced to New Castle in 1689. By 1703 the growing congregation took over the site of the old blockhouse on public land to build their church. The Presbyterians

Mid-nineteenth-century etching by Benjamin Ferris of Immanuel Episcopal Church. *(Courtesy of New Castle Historical Society)*

were not happy with this show of favoritism toward England's established church, but William Penn, fearful of losing his colony to the Calvert family of Maryland in an English court, dared not refuse.

The structure built in 1703-07 was a simple hipped-roof building that faced east toward the Holy Land. During the course of the eighteenth century the number of worshippers, especially those of wealth and prominence, increased. In 1818 the church's vestry persuaded the rising Philadelphia architect William Strickland to

Laussat Richter Rogers's etching of Immanuel Church in 1930. *(Courtesy of New Castle Historical Society)*

volunteer his services to provide plans for a much-enlarged and more sophisticated church building. The resulting additions turned the original orientation of the building around so that the nave now faced west. Transepts were also attached on either side to create a cruciform floor plan. Most prominently, Strickland added a square tower with a crenellated top on which rested a tall spire. The town added a clock and bell for public benefit. Later addi-

The burned-out shell of Immanuel Church after the fire of 1980. *(Courtesy of New Castle Historical Society)*

tions added space for the growing congregation.

On February 1, 1980, sparks from a marsh fire ignited the church roof's wooden shingles, burning the church in a huge blaze that consumed the spire and the entire interior. Despite the heroic efforts of nearly every fire company in New Castle County, the historic building

Immanuel Church's Sunday School building was the small white building to the right. *(Courtesy of New Castle Historical Society)*

with its old timber support beams became a smoldering ruin. Only the charred walls remained.

The congregation began at once to rebuild. Recognizing that the building they had lost had been altered so many times as to have lost the clarity of its design, it was decided to rebuild the church as much as possible to its appearance as Strickland had designed it in the 1820s. To prevent another tragedy, the rebuilders incorporated elements such as roof tiles made of clay and steel supports in place of timbers to make the church more structurally sound and fire resistant. The steeple was reconstructed, and the sound of its bells can be heard once again.

The churchyard cemetery contains the graves of many of old New Castle's most prominent citizens including founding father George Read, Governor Gunning Bedford, and Delaware Chancellor Kensey Johns. In addition to burials, the church used its surrounding property to build a one-story Sunday school in 1839. That building, now removed, stood in the portion of the cemetery closest to the arsenal.

When the churchyard was filled with graves, Immanuel Church created a cemetery on the Glebe Farm northeast of the town. The *glebe* was the name given to the farmland that a wealthy colonial-era parishio-

The Academy shares the Harmony Street end of the Green with Immanuel Church.

ner had provided to support the minister. Such provisions for churches and colleges were common in England and became a feature of colonial American society as well.

The Academy Adjacent to Immanuel Church stands the Academy, built to be a school in 1798-1801. It is the most architecturally significant public building built in New Castle during the post-revolutionary period. New Castle's leaders planned to build a school on that site in the early 1700s, and in 1772 the Assembly of the Lower Counties granted the land on the Green for that purpose, but the project fell victim to the uncertainties and lack of capital of the war era. Finally, in the late 1790s, thanks in large part to assistance from the Trustees of the Common, the town's leading citizens organized to construct a school to be open to those who could pay a modest tuition.

This building exhibits Federal architecture at its best. The two-story-tall and seven-bay-wide brick structure exudes a level of substance and formality based upon mathematically rendered architectural symmetry that bespoke the optimistic self-confidence of

The Academy

an expanding community in the new nation. Note the slight forward projection of the center bay, embellished by examples of restrained elegance from basement to cupola. Double doors, recessed within deep wooden panels, are topped by a fanlight surrounded by pilasters and an arch made of molded wood. A Palladian window dominates the second floor, while a circular window sits within a coved pediment at the top level. Much of the woodwork on the façade displays such sophisticated decorative details as fluting and punch-and-gouge patterns. A brick wall encloses the back of the building. Inside the front doors the original divided staircase rises from the central hallway

Federal-style details of the Academy's central bay include high-style woodworking.

to join at a landing into one. The cupola was added in 1811. Alas, records do not name the architect or master craftsman of this finely executed building.

The Academy was a private school for both boys and girls until 1852, when the state passed a public school law that required New Castle residents to pay a school tax and have a public school. The Academy remained a public school and used the Green as its school yard until 1931, when William Penn School was opened along the Basin Road.

Since then Immanuel Episcopal Church has used the building as a Sunday school under a long-term lease, now held by the State of Delaware.

The Arsenal Between 1809 and 1811 the federal government built an arsenal on the Green as part of its defensive preparations for a feared second British invasion. The one-story brick building, purpose-built with wagon entrances at both gable ends, served as a warehouse for weapons and ammunition. After the construction of Fort Delaware on Pea Patch Island, the building served as a supply center for the fort. By mid-century New Castle residents concluded that an arsenal in their midst was dangerous and demanded that the United States Army vacate the building. The army left, but the building's name has remained.

Despite the building's proximity to the jail with its occasional executions, in 1852 the arsenal was transformed into the New Castle Institute, a public school. To accommodate the number of students, a second floor was added to the arsenal.

The eagle atop a cannon reminds visitors of the Arsenal's origin.

The Arsenal

For nearly eighty years, until William Penn High School opened, it served as the town's high school. During the Great Depression, a WPA-sponsored project led by local architect Laussat Rogers removed features that had been associated with the school and restored the building to better convey the "spirit" of the early nineteenth century. A marble bas relief on the south end of the building, showing a bird (presumably an eagle) perched on top of a field gun, dates from the period when it had been an arsenal.

The Green's Many Uses

Today walking on the Green is like walking in a park. That serene sense of space and history is a recent phenomenon, for

Composite image of the three buildings, all still standing, that served as the town's school houses until the 1930s. *(Courtesy of New Castle Historical Society)*

the Green has always reflected the changing uses of the buildings on it. It is difficult to determine the degree to which the Green ever provided pasture for animals, but from early days it clearly offered open space for the towns-people. The market area decreed by Penn in 1682 brought people and brisk trade to the area on market days. Penned animals due to be sold at market were a major part of that trade.

Watercolor by Alice Hay of the Green looking toward Delaware Street. *(Courtesy of New Castle Historical Society)*

In the eighteenth century the Green was the scene for an aston-ishing range of activities. In addi-tion to the functions associated with market days and fairs, there were baptisms, weddings, and funerals at Immanuel Church. But the Green also served as the site for public punishments at the whipping post, stocks, and gallows. The first execu-tion of a female in Delaware took place on the Green in 1731, when a woman was burned to death on the scaf-fold for murdering her husband. It was also the site for colonial political life. Men who came there to attend the Assembly learned the art of governance on the path to independence. It was on the Green that bonfires were ignited to burn the Royal insignia taken from the courthouse in July 1776.

The Green might have been less tumultuous in the nineteenth century, but no less noisy. The mar-kets continued; punishment moved inside prison walls; and children's activities took over. By 1895 ornate iron fencing, made by a New Castle factory, surrounded the Green, with its decorative fountain, playground, tennis court, and basketball court.

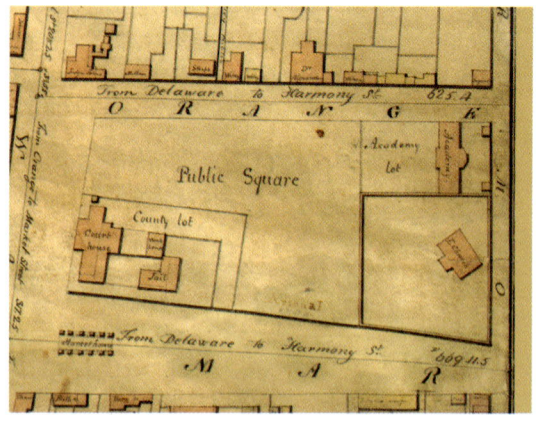

The Green and market stalls at the time of the Latrobe Survey. *(Courtesy of Delaware Public Archives)*

The Green had everything but much green grass.

The Market and Town Hall

The area that centers on cobble-stoned Market Street between Delaware Street and Harmony Street, including the Town Hall and the brick-paved and grassed plot behind it, was once the site of New Castle's town market. Penn's government established a weekly market there in 1682 to provide an organized way for farmers to sell their produce

A two-tier structure for stocks (above) and whipping post (below) stands in the middle of the prison yard as inmates break rocks around it. Note the proximity to the Arsenal, then a school, in the background. *(Courtesy of New Castle Historical Society)*

and animals to people who lived nearby or who were arriving or departing by ship. In 1729 the General Assembly extended the market to two days a week: Wednesdays and Saturdays. An elected clerk of the market ensured that the rules for weights and measures, prices and payments, and the proper impounding of animals were maintained. By 1800 the clerk was also charged to rent stalls in the frame market house that appears in the Latrobe Survey of 1804-05.

The early market house proved inadequate by the 1820s. It was small and frequently needed repair. Since the town's government needed a home, the Trustees of the Common agreed in 1823 to construct a town hall of brick that would serve as a head house to be connected to a new market house. The combined structures were similar in some respects to connected markets and head houses in Philadelphia, except that the New Castle market stalls were made of wood

Drawing of Market House from the Latrobe Survey. *(Courtesy of Delaware Public Archives)*

REMAINS THAT RECALL THE NEW CASTLE AND FRENCHTOWN RAILROAD

Although the New Castle and Frenchtown Railroad is long gone, it left several remains. A pyramid-shaped stone monument to the railroad was erected in 1915 behind the Town Hall on Second Street. The monument is constructed of stones that were once used as sleepers, or ties, along the track. Additional stone sleepers, with their trademark drilled holes, can be seen amid the brick pavers in alleys on The Strand and on Delaware Street. The use of stone to hold the railroad tracks seemed appropriate in the early days of railroad building. Experience showed, however, that their rigidity presented problems, and they were soon replaced by the wooden railroad ties that we know today. Once removed, the sleepers found other uses.

The railroad's original ticket office located in Battery Park is another remnant from the New Castle and Frenchtown Railroad. When the Pennsylvania Railroad took over ownership of the NC and FTRR, the little building was removed to another location to be used as a flagman's booth. In 1946, in derelict condition, it was put in storage. It was rescued in 1953 and restored to become the historic attraction one sees today in New Castle.

Painting by Robert Montgomery Bird of Market House at the rear of Town Hall looking toward Delaware Street. Bird, a talented artist, author, and playwright, was descended from several prominent local families and as a boy lived in a house on Delaware Street. Bird was 20 years old when he painted this view in 1826. *(Courtesy of Robert Montgomery Bird)*

instead of more permanent brick. Today, the only remaining part of the New Castle structure is the brick part—the Town Hall. The frame building was demolished in the late nineteenth century, but its ghost can be seen behind the Town Hall in the brick pavement on which it sat. The discolored bricks in the rear of the Town Hall reveal traces of where the frame market structure was once joined to it.

In 1897 the introduction of electric trolleys linking Wilmington to New Castle gave local people the opportunity to purchase food in the larger city's market and helped doom the market in New Castle. In its place the Trustees of the Common created in 1898 a park to run behind the Town Hall. Fittingly, the park is home to the Charles Parks statue of William Penn and also to a monument to the New Castle and Frenchtown Railroad.

New Castle and Frenchtown Railroad Marker is made of original sleepers, or stones used to hold the railroad track in place. *(Courtesy of Hagley Museum and Library)*

As the head house of the market and the center of town government, the Town Hall was more central to the daily lives of most residents of New Castle than was the county courthouse nearby. The Town Hall was designed to be taken seriously. This almost square structure stands three full stories tall and is capped by a hipped roof that supports a three-tiered cupola, which stands taller than the cupola at the apex of its neighbor, the courthouse.

The most conspicuous feature of the Town Hall's ground floor is the central arched arcade, large enough for a wagon to pass through, that was designed to be the entrance to the market. The two smaller arched rooms on either side of the arcade became the home for the town's fire equipment, which included, after 1824, a hand-pumped fire engine. When the fire equipment outgrew the space and moved elsewhere, those first floor rooms were rented to businesses, including at one time a barber shop and a meat market. Now it houses the town newspaper.

The second floor of the Town Hall continues to fulfill its original purpose as the meeting place for the town council. The third floor of the Town Hall is also home to the Trustees of the Common, whose largesse made the building affordable. It was originally intended to accommodate lodge meetings, but that function moved to the newly built Opera House on Delaware Street in 1880.

In today's automobile age, New Castle residents shop for food at big-box grocery stores located in strip malls along suburban highways, no longer

Town Hall today. The statue of William Penn can be seen through the building's central arch. *(Courtesy of Carlo Viola)*

needing colonial market stalls. Yet while the market house has disappeared, the Town Hall continues to serve New Castle as a seat of local government.

DELAWARE STREET

From Courthouse to River

William Penn's decision to place a courthouse and jail on the Green set in motion the transfer of the locus of political and judicial power and activity from Harmony Street to Delaware Street. Thus, a once peripheral street became the town's spine. A map that reconstructs the town's layout at the time of Penn's arrival in 1682 shows some early Dutch and English land purchases and construction on the western end of New Castle, but, with the coming of the courthouse in 1687, property across the street from the courthouse lot increased in value for use as residences, inns, and taverns. Early buyers and sellers included established townspeople from the days of the Dutch colony as well as enterprising Philadelphians, including William Markham, Penn's first cousin and a leader in establishing the Quaker colony.

In the Penn era Delaware Street became a mixed-use area where residences and commerce intermingled—sometimes in adjacent structures but often in buildings that themselves served multiple purposes. By the early twentieth century Delaware Street had become the center of New Castle's commercial activity, mostly for locals, but the street also included hotels to accommodate visitors. The post-World-War-II automobile era changed the nature of business yet again. Today small specialty stores, restaurants, and offices share

110 Delaware Street.

space with residences. Apartments have replaced the earlier inns and hotels, but the tourist trade remains integral to the businesses of Delaware Street.

Portions of at least eight eighteenth-century buildings still stand along the oldest part of Delaware Street from the river to Third Street, but those colonial-era structures are often hidden from view behind new facades and other expansions. Two beautiful survivors can be seen at numbers 110 and 214. The house at Number 110 dates from the mid to late eighteenth century, with elements of an even earlier age, such as a beehive oven, incorporated into the house. Georgian in style, it features a water table, belt course, denticulated cornice, brick laid in Flemish bond, and elegant proportions. It is four bays in width, a size common in larger cities such as Philadelphia but uncommon in New Castle. Like many early buildings this structure served as both a workshop and a house.

Side view of 110 Delaware Street.

The house at Number 212 has had a long and convoluted history. It consists of three distinct sections that span nearly 150 years and provides a mini-architectural lesson in itself. The first section to the right of the doorway was built on land that passed through the hands of at least seven owners in the course of sixty years. Sylvester Garland, a merchant and innkeeper, bought the land in about 1719 and built a house for his daughter and son-in-law, the Presbyterian minister. This first section is a fine early example of the Georgian style of architecture. Its brickwork, including a belt course and relieving arches above the window openings, is impressive.

212 Delaware Street.

As imposing as the house might have been and however central its location, owners came and went quickly, often losing the property to debt. Title to the house changed thirteen times before the second section of the house, to the left, was added in the 1790s by James Booth, Sr. In addition to the obvious change in brickwork, the door was moved, which gives the expanded dwelling a very un-Georgian asymmetry at ground level. The Federal-style cornice does its best to pull the sections together. The interior also reflects the high-style woodworking and decoration of the Federal era. The third portion of frame was added as a law office in the 1860s.

As the size of Number 212 changed, so did its uses as a residence and/or inn. It is often called the Booth House because the longest period of ownership was that of several generations of the Booth family, distinguished lawyers, judges, and government officials. It was from this house that Maria Booth Rogers wrote her account of the fire on the Strand in 1824.

Detail of 212 Delaware Street shows differences in brickwork between the 1790s section, left, and the 1720s portion, right.

Well into the nineteenth century the first two blocks of Delaware Street moving north from the river continued to be filled in with structures ranging from the modest-sized units of Cloud's Row (numbers 117-23) to the Terry House at Number 130. Built in about 1865, this large brick house, which stylistically nods to the Federal, Greek Revival, and even Italianate styles, is anything but modest.

130 Delaware Street.

Back wing of 130 Delaware Street.

The house commands attention because of its size and architectural details such as a sandstone water table, linked chimneys rising from each end wall, and the deep, corbelled brick cornice of the front façade. A two-story gallery running the full length of the long rear wing provides river views and breezes. The house did, in fact, require such a large number of bricks that some local wags nicknamed it "Terry's Folly." Howell Terry, a wealthy banker, built the house at the end of his career, but he did not enjoy it for long. In less than two decades it had passed out of the family.

The pattern of use and adaptive use begun in the eighteenth century has continued to the present time. Buildings have come down or gone up, been altered, renovated, and expanded to meet changing commercial and/or residential needs. In about the middle of the nineteenth century, merchants began installing plate-glass shop windows. Today the street contains examples of small early display windows as well as modern full-front plate glass. Number 120 provides an example of an early nineteenth-century building where shop windows were installed at the end of that century.

Adding a plate-glass window was a modest alteration compared to more extensive changes undertaken in the next block. Numbers 202-04 began as an eighteenth-century inn. Originally a two-floor building, it gained a third floor in 1847 and a new brick front after World War II. Its neighbor at

Two views of changes in brickwork over three centuries on Delaware Street: 204, left, and 206, right. Sometimes the changes are in clear view, while other times plaster and advertising cover the surfaces. *(Left, courtesy of Carlo Viola, photographer)*

Number 206 probably dates to the early eighteenth century. After the Civil War its original gambrel roof was changed to a low gable that increased space on the top floor. The building has also been re-fronted with modern machine-made bricks. While the original buildings have both been altered beyond recognition, suggestions of their past can be seen in the brickwork along their sides. That is where you will find the old bricks, so different

View of Delaware Street about 1900 with early storefronts and open-air trolley. *(Courtesy of New Castle Historical Society)*

in size, color, and method of laying from the new section. Buildings, like people, always leave tell-tale reminders after facelifts.

Two other buildings in the 200 block of Delaware Street present strong challenges to the sleuthing skills of early-house detectives. Today the structure at Number 210 is a bank, but in the early eighteenth century it was an inn and tavern with a back wing and stable reached by a wide-arched opening, giving it the look and feel of an English coaching inn that offered stagecoach travelers food and accommodations. Repairs and alterations after the Civil War added a Victorian patina to the façade, but major structural changes came with Prohibition, when the tavern gave way to stores. In the process, the building lost its archway but gained dormers and plate-glass display windows. The last major change to the façade came in about 1970, when a bank took over the property and replaced the store front of the grocery with a colonial-style look that exposed the still-extant belt course and the old arched

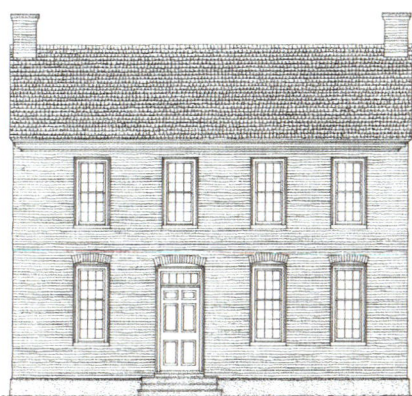 

The evolution of a building: 210 Delaware Street. *(Top left, courtesy of M & T Bank; top right and bottom left, courtesy of New Castle Historical Society; and bottom left, courtesy of Carlo Viola, photographer)*

stable passage. Once again, bricks have a story to tell. A display inside the bank shows the deep well that once served the old inn.

At the end of the block, Number 216 dates back to the first half of the eighteenth century when it was an inn and then a residence. Early changes removed an old kitchen wing and replaced it with a modern extension to the house. Late in the nineteenth century came shops, followed in the early twentieth century by massive alterations that completely transformed a house with stores into an hotel. Today the building at the corner of Delaware and Third streets still has its nineteenth-century gambrel roof, but apartments that now share space with offices and a restaurant have replaced hotel rooms.

The latest renovations to Number 216 have sought to suggest the earlier look or feel of the building, a restoration process that has been on-going in the community since the 1920s. All of the units of Cloud's Row that face Delaware Street, for example, have been returned to their original appearance,

222 Delaware Street before its transformation into an hotel in the early twentieth century. This building, as well as its neighbor at number 220, were proposed for demolition on the Perry, Shaw and Hepburn Map A. *(Courtesy of New Castle Historical Society)*

and those that had once been turned into shops, including a Chinese laundry, are again residences.

The building at Number 220 is an anomaly: a modern, purpose-built structure. Constructed in the early twentieth century in the Beaux Arts style to be a bank, it now serves as the administrative center for the town of New Castle. The building includes large round-arched windows, two-story stone pilasters topped by a stone frieze, and a denticulated cornice. Its style nods to classicism but blends in with the older buildings that surround it. Had it been built any time after the rise of the Colonial Revival movement in New Castle, which took root just a few years later, it would no doubt look less classically grand and more Georgian.

From Third Street to the Ferry Cut-Off

The 300 and 400 blocks of Delaware Street present a clear architectural manifestation of the town's economic shift from an economy of trade to one of industry. Here stand the imposing houses of the interrelated Johns and Van Dyke families, members of the town's political and legal elite into the nineteenth century. Those houses are all architectural gems and, with the exception of the

220 Delaware Street, built in the early twentieth century, was originally a bank. It is now the administrative center for New Castle town government. From Perry, Shaw and Hepburn photograph, 1946. *(Courtesy of New Castle Historical Society)*

Kensey Johns, Jr., house at the corner of Delaware and West Fourth streets, have already been described for their distinguished embodiment of the late Georgian and Federal periods of architecture. Those same two blocks also contain the dominating Second-Empire-style Opera House and two houses built at the end of the west side of the 400 block for two of the town's new

Looking up Delaware Street from Third Street, early twentieth century. *(Courtesy of Delaware Historical Society)*

leaders of nineteenth-century New Castle's business and industry, James G. Shaw and William Herbert. Both men built houses of a size to rival their earlier counterparts down the block, but in a different style.

Some of Shaw's three-story house can still be seen, now incorporated into the extension of New Castle's new library that opened in 2010. As a mill owner and real-estate developer, Shaw chose to build a large house that was dignified but not showy. Shaw's neighbor William Herbert was a politician and businessman who made his wealth as a skilled machinist. He built a tall, three-story brick house in the Italianate style with flat roof, bracketed

Herbert Mansion on Delaware Street at Fifth Street was torn down to build the public library in the 1960s. *(Courtesy of New Castle Historical Society)*

cornice, and front porch plus a less tall, two-story rear wing with an elaborately ornamented one-story wooden porch. It was a large house sufficient to accommodate a family with ten children. Herbert died in 1895, and by 1912 the house had passed out of the family and into the possession of Saint Peter's Roman Catholic Church. The church adapted the house for use as a convent, which the nuns considered very "elegant." When the church built a new convent on its school complex on Harmony at Fifth Street in the 1960s, the old Herbert house was torn down to make way for the public library. Where the Herbert house once stood is now a

William Herbert. *(Courtesy of New Castle Historical Society)*

22,000 square-foot modern facility that combines the new with the old Shaw house. The new portion itself displays echos of the Romanesque arches of the late-nineteenth-century firehouse that stood on South Street between Fifth and Sixth streets.

The 300 and 400 blocks of Delaware Street are also the last of the blocks that contain a substantial mix of commercial and residential structures.

Compare the buildings at numbers 318, 414, and 431. The first is an eighteenth-century building converted to shops at ground level in the 1880s. The second is a late-nineteenth-century building that is commercial on the ground level with living quarters above. The third dates to the 1880s, with a late-nineteenth-century

The store at 318 Delaware Street was built in the eighteenth century as a residence.

addition. At the time the Herbert family lived across the street, it was known as the "Marble Hall" because it was the workshop and stable of a tombstone maker. The buildings could not be more different, but each demonstrates the same mixed-use principle that has operated on Delaware Street for several centuries.

Most of the buildings along Delaware Street from the 400 block to the highway are vernacular in style. Builders of every era often combine elements of various currently fashionable architectural styles to create a common local style. The craftsmen of New Castle and the surrounding area have left us with a full range of vernacular expressions of the Georgian and Federal, Greek Revival, Italianate, Second Empire, Queen Anne, and Colonial Revival styles as well as hybrids that mix elements of each so as to merit their own category: composite style.

500 block of Delaware Street.

The majority of the houses in the 500 block date from the late nineteenth century. Some were built to be single houses, while others are joined. Most are two stories tall and two or three bays wide. Roofs might be gabled with or without dormers, flat, or mansard, and most have bracketed cornices. A good number have open or enclosed porches. The Queen Anne building at Number 531, built in 1885, is a good vernacular example with its cross-gable roof, doorway with a pediment, and stained glass windows.

531 Delaware Street, built in 1885, in the Queen Anne style.

Similarly, the United States Post Office at Number 501 exemplifies a Colonial Revival-style public building. Built in the Great Depression as a WPA project, it provided the first permanent location for mail delivery since 1683, when postal service to the town began. The building, with its cupola, keystone-topped arches above the windows, and fanlight over the main door, fits well into its surroundings. Inside there is a wall mural painted in 1938 by J. Scott Williams that rather fancifully illustrates William Penn's arrival in New Castle. Williams was born in England but spent most of his life as an artist living in

Post Office under construction, 1935. *(Courtesy of New Castle Historical Society)*

New York and northern New Jersey. The mural, however, was not a WPA project. It came to the new post office under a program of the Department of the Treasury that found good quality art to be purchased for post offices whenever funds became available. Across the street from the post office is a row of late twentieth-century Colonial Revival townhouses that replaced a movie theater, which in turn had been constructed from the shell of a nineteenth-century commercial building.

If the post office building's style has proven to be compatible with the aesthetic of Delaware's colonial capital, a second government building, the last on the street, is incongruous in style. The Van Dyke Armory, built in 1917 on the eve of America's entry into World War I, is typical of armories then being built all over the country. It was designed in a castellated style replete with battlements and buttresses more reminiscent of an Italian hill town than of a town on the Delaware River.

Undoubtedly, the most dominant property along upper Delaware Street is the Methodist Church and its adjacent cemetery, located on the west side of Fifth Street. The church, built at the height of the Civil War in 1863, combines modified elements of Gothic Revival and Second Empire styles with the solidity and simplicity that characterized Methodism.

The first missionary of the Methodist faith in Delaware was a retired English army officer, Captain Thomas Webb, who travelled through the American colonies in the 1760s. When he was denied permission to preach in the New Castle Courthouse, Captain Webb preached in the tavern and inn of Robert Furness, a Methodist convert, who is known as the "Father of Methodism" in New Castle. About a decade later Francis Asbury, another major

Methodist Church.

founder of Methodism, also preached at Furness's establishment. The tavern stood at 210 Delaware Street, the current location of a bank.

In a town dominated by Episcopalians and Presbyterians, Methodism only slowly attracted followers in New Castle. Its early adherents included African Americans as well as whites. In 1820 the number of Methodists had grown sufficiently to purchase the property where the present church is located and to build a small Meeting House on a portion of the present cemetery. In 1857 the black members withdrew to found a separate congregation, Mount Salem Methodist Episcopal Church, on East Fourth Street. Other African-American Methodists had formed their own church, Union Methodist Church, on the west side of town decades earlier.

By 1863 New Castle was home to an ever-increasing number of Methodists. Some worked for the railroad, while others worked at the mills that were becoming the town's major employers. The most important newcomer was Thomas Tasker, the entrepreneur whose investments in New Castle were so important to its industrial development. Tasker was a devout Methodist. Although he continued to live in Philadelphia, he made frequent trips to New Castle, where he worshipped and even preached in the Methodist Church. It is not surprising, therefore, to note that the Methodists had the funds to build the church at 510 Delaware Street one year after Tasker

FRANCIS ASBURY IN NEW CASTLE

Francis Asbury, the founder of the Methodist Church in America, stopped in New Castle many times on his preaching journeys up and down the East Coast. His journal entry for his first visit on April 9, 1772, provides a rare glimpse into the town's social and religious dynamics on the eve of the American Revolution. Just as Captain Benjamin Webb, another early evangelist, had found earlier, nearly all of New Castle's doors were closed to his preaching.

... rode on to Newcastle, and stopped at the house of brother Furness, a tavernkeeper, but a good man. Preached there to a few people, but met with opposition, and found the Methodists had done no great good. The court house here is shut against us; but it opens for dances and balls; and brother Furness has lost his company by receiving us. However we were comforted together.

Perhaps Robert Furness, then owner of the inn at 210 Delaware Street, lost business in the short run, but he lived on for many years in New Castle, rising to be a very wealthy citizen in the new nation.

—*The Journals and Letters of Francis Asbury, vol. 1, p. 73.*

had become a major figure in the town's economy. Over the years the congregation continued to grow, adding a Sunday school wing in 1876 and a Fellowship Hall in 1956. The church also added a parsonage across the street at Number 532, as the prominent stone doorbell surround announces.

Doorway to the Methodist Church on Delaware Street.

Visitors to the parsonage could be sure they were at the right house when they rang the doorbell at the left of the door.

Census and other data suggest that in the era of New Castle's industrialization, the residents of Delaware Street were less diverse ethnically and racially than were those on the east or west sides of the town that Delaware Street divides. The overwhelming majority were white and native-born, largely from Delaware or the surrounding states of New Jersey, Pennsylvania, and Maryland. Only a small number of immigrants lived on Delaware Street, with the largest group coming from Ireland. Most of the Irish residents had a skill, either in the crafts or in industry, but there was also a bartender and some servants. A smaller number of immigrants came from England, and all of them had skilled occupations. Most immigrants lived between Fourth and Sixth streets, although some boarded around Second and Market. Any African Americans living on Delaware Street resided in the households of their employers. Most, but not all, were females.

Much has changed on Delaware Street in the last century. The trolley no longer runs along the street to bring shoppers to the town's business district or to convey residents to the stores and businesses of Wilmington. Automobiles have expanded the potential for shopping, employment, and housing far beyond the town's

532 Delaware Street once served as the Methodist parsonage.

center. Today Delaware Street remains New Castle's spine. It retains the look and feel of the past while it adjusts to an ever-changing world.

THE HISTORIC CENTER:
THE STRAND THROUGH FOURTH BETWEEN
DELAWARE AND HARMONY STREETS

The Strand

This one street dates back to the earliest years of Dutch settlement outside Fort Casimir and has been called variously First Row, Front Street, Water Street, and The Strand. Development started on the land side of the street. After 1700, when riverside or bank lots became available in the first block, development expanded to both sides of the street. Today people prize The Strand for its water views, but earlier generations valued the water itself as an engine of transportation and commerce.

Looking up The Strand from Delaware Street. By J.B. Moll, Jr. *(Courtesy of New Castle Historical Society)*

Today this block of The Strand projects the architectural homogeneity of a quiet and serene residential street. But that's not how it looked in previous centuries. In earlier times people lived on The Strand, but they shared the space with hotels, taverns, workshops, warehouses, and businesses engaged in trade, transport, and even manufacturing. Activity swirled up and down the street, both night and day, ensuring that this was a lively, noisy, sometimes even rowdy area. Important people, including lawyers, government officials, and businessmen who engaged in international trade shared space with craftsmen, innkeepers, travelers passing through New Castle and the assorted laborers, servants, and slaves who worked there. The latter group might live with their masters or employers, but sometimes they lived elsewhere.

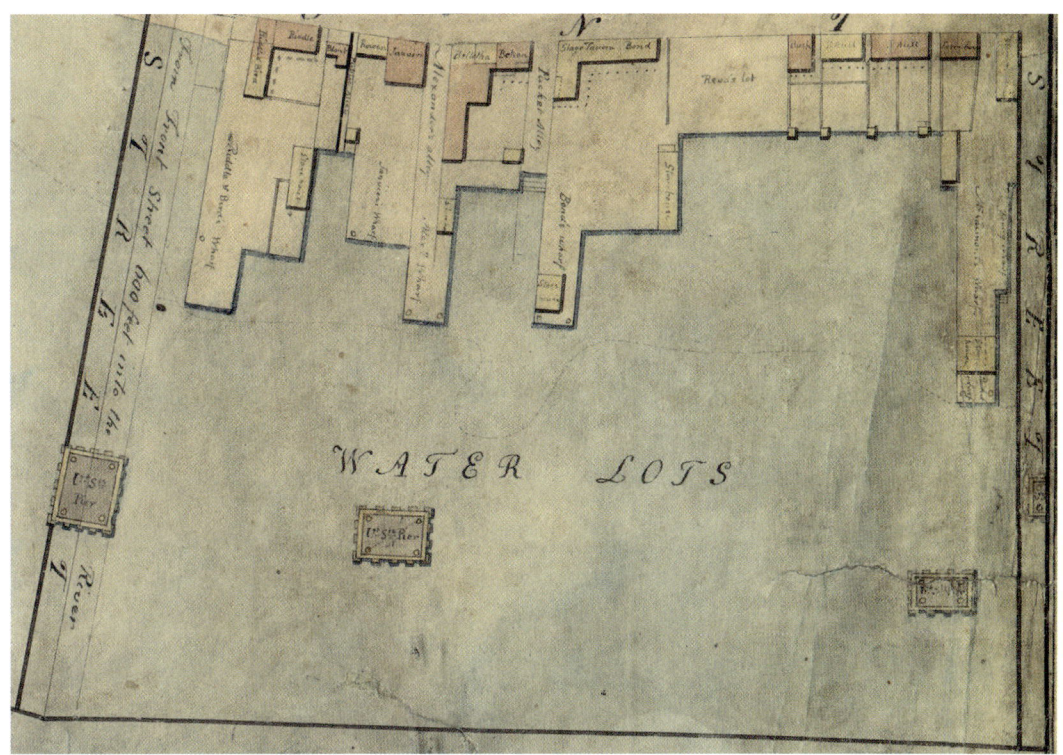

This detail from the Latrobe Survey of buildings and wharves along The Strand between Delaware and Harmony streets includes three of the town's ice piers. *(Courtesy of Delaware Public Archives)*

From the eighteenth century into the nineteenth century, New Castle's trade and transportation centered along The Strand from Delaware Street to Harmony Street, as did the wharves and warehouses of a water-based economy. Probably no wharves existed before the time of William Penn, but by the time of the Latrobe Survey there were four major wharves. Here large ships engaged in international and inter-coastal trade as well as smaller, more local vessels tied up to load and unload cargo. Packet boats also picked up and dropped passengers as well as cargo and mail on a regular schedule.

Packet boats, first sail and then steam, stopped at the wharf on Packet Alley. Today a stable dating to the first half of the nineteenth century, now transformed into a house, remains as the only physical connection to that era of transportation. The stable, like others in backyards nearer Delaware Street, now gone, was needed by the stage line and then by the railroad that followed it, as part of a Philadelphia-Baltimore land/sea route. Another ferry

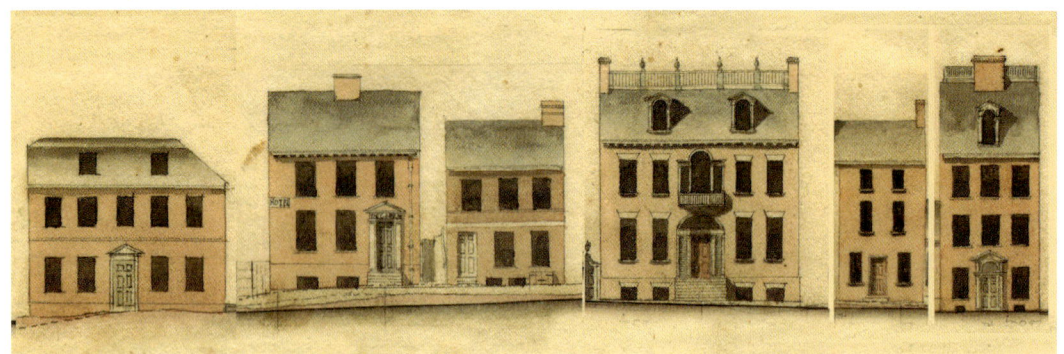

Six houses built before the fire of 1824 still stand on the land side of The Strand. From the Latrobe Survey. *(Courtesy of Delaware Public Archives)*

operated at the wharf at the foot of Harmony and The Strand. This ferry was a government-authorized monopoly dating from the early eighteenth century that carried passengers back and forth across the Delaware River between New Castle and Salem, New Jersey. The Latrobe Survey shows the ferry house at what is now 57 The Strand.

For the merchants a noisy and busy area meant business, but danger always lurked in the combination of frame warehouses and houses. Disaster materialized on the afternoon of April 26, 1824, when a roaring inferno started in the lumber sheds of Jeremiah Bowman, located near the river and wharfs behind what is today Number 9. Fueled by a strong wind, flames raced up-river, jumping back and forth to engulf most of the houses on both sides of the street before being stopped at Number 42 and Number 49. In all, twenty-three houses, numerous warehouses, and outbuildings were consumed by flames.

Doorways to 53 and 55 The Strand.

Fortunately ten houses built before the fire still stand, four (numbers 2, 5, 6, 8) at the south end of the street and six at the north end (numbers 42, 49, 53, 55, 56, and 100 Harmony). These buildings—altered, re-altered, and re-re-altered in some cases—range from pre-Revolutionary Georgian houses such as numbers

Parish House at Harmony and The Strand.

2, 6, and 8, to a late-eighteenth-century frame survivor at Number 49 and a modest brick at Number 56, owned by the doctor who operated the ferry service located across the street. In addition to the magnificent Federal-style Read House described in the Architecture section, early nineteenth-century survivors include the double house at numbers 53 and 55, the most stylishly constructed work known to have been done by house builder John Aull. He built these dwellings for his and his brother's families.

Another major example of the Federal style stands at 100 Harmony Street, built at the same time and by the same master carpenter as the Read House. Charles Thomas contracted with Peter Crouding in 1801 to build a three-and-a-half-story brick hotel/residence adjacent to the wharf at Harmony Street. With three bays along The Strand and six along Harmony, the double-entry building boasts fine Federal styling at the doorways, around the windows, and at the cornice line—all topped by a widow's walk. Crouding provided Thomas with the same level of crafts-

Harmony Street wharf and The Strand, probably late nineteenth century. *(Courtesy of New Castle Historical Society)*

manship he gave Read. The quality of materials and high level of workmanship suggest an owner with high ambitions.

Rebuilding after the fire began almost immediately. Most buildings were total losses, but portions of some could be saved or salvaged and incorporated into new foundations or buildings, as can be seen in basements, attics, or during renovations. Rebuilding provided the opportunity to change building material from wood to brick and to reposition and even expand the size of some of the structures. Most builders and owners chose both options. The rebuilding process also provided an opportunity to build in the more avant-garde architectural styles being championed by the new architects of America, including the very men who had produced the town survey of 1805. No one along The Strand chose that more modern course. New Castilians clearly preferred to retain the more conservative, tried-and-true Federal style. The lovely, large Federal-style townhouse at Number 17, for example, rose in brick over the ruins of a frame house that had been part of a four-generation-old complex of workshops and warehouses.

Advertising remains on the Packet Alley side of 25 The Strand long after the store became a residence. *(Courtesy of Carlo Viola)*

Several men built more than one house on the block. Jeremiah Bowman, the lumberman and carpenter, whose shed was ground zero for the fire, built numbers 9, 13, and 15, all in brick, and merchant James McCullough built Number 30 for himself and Number 25 for a shop. He also built numbers 27, 29, 31, and 33 as rental units. This row of four brick houses reflects both careful attention to materials and craftsmanship balanced with a restrained simplicity in design.

Some of the buildings arising from the ashes of 1824 were designed to be businesses and others to be business-residence combinations. Number 25 on the north side of Packet Alley always intrigues people because of the advertisement painted on the side of the alley wall. From earliest days this site had been commercial—first as a tavern, then a ship chandlery, and later a general store. It became a house only in the mid-twentieth century.

Businesses lasted longest on the river side of The Strand at both ends of the block. The Truss brothers, Samuel and James, built the double house at numbers 57 and 59 The Strand about 1870, where the old ferry house had once stood. They expanded the adjacent wharf area for their businesses as grain and coal dealers. At the other end of the street stood Number 4, constructed in 1850-51 as a bank, while its older neighbor across the street, Number 5, continued to expand in size after the fire of 1824. Today known as the Jefferson House, it served for many years as the house and store of Elihu Jefferson. Warehouses and sheds for the business stood on the side and behind the brick structure near its wharf. Eventually the building became an hotel with dining facilities and dancehall pavilion on the rear. It began a downward spiral that ended only when Philip and Lydia Laird bought the building and converted it into apartments just before the outbreak of World War II.

Indeed, only as the boats, the stage, and railroad ceased to need The Strand location and as the town's center of trade and commerce moved elsewhere, did The Strand evolve over the course of the twentieth century into the residential neighborhood it is today. Now only the automobile intrudes on its quiet serenity.

At first glance, the architecture of the second block of The Strand might seem incongruous, but it actually serves as a continuation of a timeline of architectural styles. The continuum begins with the house on the

Jefferson House, with its open-air dance pavillion facing the river. *(Courtesy of New Castle Historical Society)*

northwest corner, a frame mid-Victorian-style double house, and then jumps directly to the twentieth century. The styles range from a modest, hipped-roof bungalow through mid-century Colonial Revivals to very recent grand houses created with some references to design elements of earlier eras, but mostly designed

The Strand looking east from Delaware Street. *(Courtesy of Carlo Viola)*

to enjoy unobstructed river views. That view could not be more different from earlier times, as an adjacent picture vividly illustrates.

Second Street from Delaware to Harmony

Second Street began as a cart path separating the block-deep lots running from The Strand, or First Row, and the Market Plaine or Green. The oldest building along the street today is the Presbyterian Church, built in 1707. Originally, the church entrance faced toward a walkway that led to The Strand. Soon other buildings were built along the cart path between the church and Delaware Street. Most of those buildings, including "a mansion house," are now gone, except for segments that remain as part of the foundations of the buildings that replaced them. Only two houses, those at numbers 15 and 17, set slightly back from the street, remain from the early nineteenth century, although it is hard to recognize them after façade and structural changes. Some have dated these houses as far back as the late eighteenth century, but if the Latrobe map is to be believed, they were built after 1805. The Latrobe map shows a street divided into four parts: two brick buildings bearing company names between Cloud's Row and Church Alley; the church, its burying grounds, and a stagecoach stable; the rear of the George Read, Sr., and George Read, Jr., properties, which are the only lots still running the full

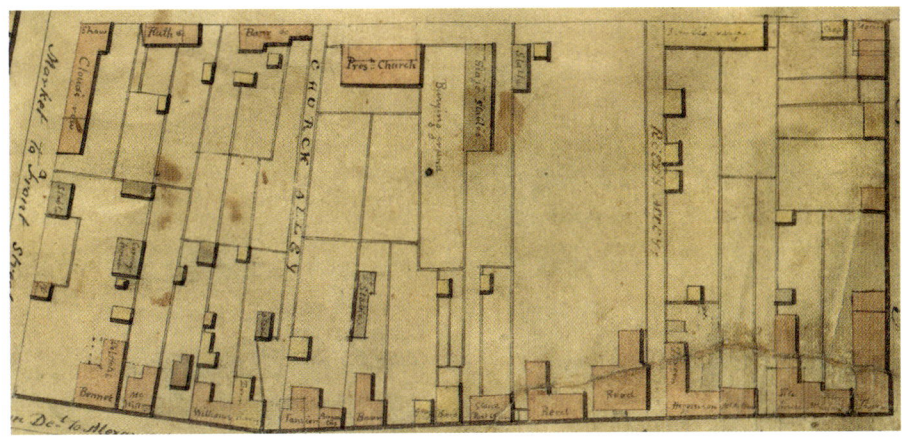

The Strand and East Second Street from Delaware Street to Harmony Street as depicted on the Latrobe Survey. *(Courtesy of Delaware Public Archives)*

depth of the block; and Aull's Row plus a small shop at the end of the block between Read's Alley and Harmony Street.

In the decades after Latrobe completed his survey in 1804-05 more houses and businesses filled in empty spaces or replaced earlier structures. The portion of Second Street from the corner with Delaware Street to the Presbyte-

Turn-of-the-twentieth-century view of Second and Delaware streets. *(Courtesy of New Castle Historical Society)*

rian Church became an important part of New Castle's central shopping district. Butcher shops, bakeries, drug stores, dry-goods and millinery stores, a bank, an undertaker's parlor, and even a billiards hall claimed space there at one time or another. Those stores, which stood across from the market stalls, continued the street's commercial heritage that dated back to the original market prescribed by William Penn.

The most dramatic embodiment of the rise of commerce along the first block of Second Street was a Second Empire building with mansard roof, elaborate shop fronts at street level, and residential space above. The removal of that building for a pocket park left only one store window as a reminder of the days when the trolley ran along the street and stores drew shoppers to the area. Now this section of Second Street is residential, except for the corner shop in Cloud's Row.

Few looking at the houses would know the complex, even confusing past that lies under those nineteenth-century structures. Just one example might encourage a closer look here— and throughout the town—for clues to a building's distant but not totally lost origin. Number 13 combines two sepa-

Greenbaum's store, 7 East Second Street, early twentieth century. A pocket park has replaced this Second-Empire building. *(Courtesy of New Castle Historical Society)*

rate buildings, a two-story commercial building (formerly Number 11) and a three-story residence, into one. Both date from about 1870, confirmed by a chimney pot on Number 13 dated *1871*. Peeling back layers of Number 13,

a fine, flat-roofed Italianate with bracketed cornice and transom-topped front door, reveals a piazza and kitchen from about 1850 and an early eighteenth-century cellar kitchen.

The remainder of the block is a study of both change and continuity over time. Despite the seeming appearance of timelessness, the Presbyterian Church's property has seen its share of changes: the rise and fall of a nineteenth-century

Sketch of 11 and 13 East Second Street. *(Courtesy of New Castle Historical Society)*

Streetscape along East Second Street of post-Civil War facades. Numbers 11 and 13 are in the center. Perry, Shaw and Hepburn photograph, late 1940s. *(Courtesy of New Castle Historical Society)*

brownstone church; the removal of a graveyard and a tennis court; and the building of an education center in the 1950s. Beyond the church, much less has been altered in the past two hundred years. The great plot of land and mansion house of George Read, Jr., remains behind a brick wall. William Couper, who made his fortune in China and then returned to New Castle, was the second owner of the house. He had lived for a time as a child in the house of George Read, Sr., before it burned in the Fire of 1824. Couper developed the mansion's extensive grounds as gardens. Like his friend Dr. Lesley, who lived on the then-outskirts of town, Couper incorporated specimen plants from around the world into his garden.

Between Read's Alley and Harmony Street, John Aull built a row of three frame houses described earlier in the Architecture section. Labeled as Aull's Range on the Latrobe survey, they were built at the beginning of the nineteenth century. A fourth frame house rose next door in about 1820, replacing an earlier frame store. It was then, and is now, the last house on the block to face Second Street. Those four houses have, of course, changed over time as succeeding generations of owners have adapted the build-

Aull's Row with shop-front windows in number 51 that date to the early twentieth century when a bakery operated in the building.

C.B. Weggermann's store at 53 East Second Street near Harmony Street, probably late nineteenth century. The family had operated a shoe business in New Castle since at least 1870. *(Courtesy of New Castle Historical Society)*

ings to meet contemporary needs. Most changes are in the rear and can be seen from Read's Alley. The only altered façade is Number 51. This occurred in the late nineteenth century when the building operated as a bakery and then as a confectioner's shop.

Second Street is an amazing street for the span of history its streetscape encompasses. In just one block there is a sweep of time from early eighteenth-century beginnings to an era of stores and commerce to the creation of a modern Sunday school and office space. Today all of the buildings, except for the church and one shop, are residences; and all of the owners, including the Presbyterian congregation, seek to preserve the unique heritages of the buildings that for a time are theirs.

East Third Street from Delaware Street to Harmony Street

The block of Third Street that faces the Green has been largely residential in character since the early nineteenth century. While residents and businesses on Second Street faced to market stalls, the walls of a jail, an arsenal, and a church yard, those who lived parallel to them on Third Street looked out on the more park-like side of the Market Plaine, or Green. The one notable exception to this otherwise residential block is the hexagon-shaped library, which is described in the Architecture section. It was built in 1892 by Philadelphia architect William Masters Camac to blend in with its surroundings while at the same time making an architectural statement for its time.

Like all of the blocks within the historic core of New Castle, the first block of Third Street between Delaware and Harmony streets originally contained a mix of houses and shops for craftsmen. Remains of earliest New Castle can be found within the foundations of some buildings that stand today. The oldest structure on the block is the Dutch House. Even that structure, which dates to the late 1690s, replaced a yet earlier building. This iconic house with its many alterations is described in detail in the Architecture section.

Postcard image titled "The School Green, New Castle, Del." shows a peaceful scene with mature trees, benches, and fountain. The only intrusion into this bucolic turn-of-the-century view is the prison wall on the far right. *(Courtesy of New Castle Historical Society)*

The Latrobe survey of 1805 shows a street of fourteen structures, about half brick and half frame. The three largest brick structures are still standing, all built to be the homes of professional men. The Kensey Johns house on the corner has already been described in the Architecture section, as has the Archibald Alexander double house. The third of those houses, Number 18, was built by John Wiley, an up-and-coming young lawyer, in 1801.

The Wiley house is four stories tall and three bays wide. The house is a fine example of a refined and restrained detached townhouse built in the new Federal style in New Castle. Its construction has often been attributed to Philadelphia master carpenter Peter Crouding, who was directing the con-

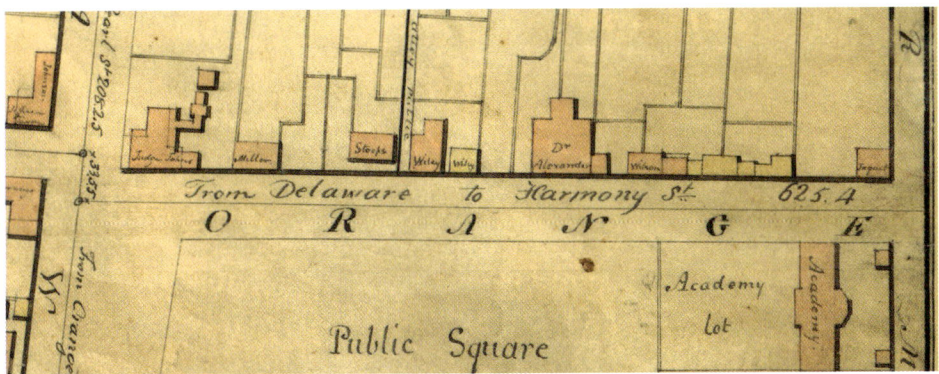

East Third Street facing the Green in 1804-05. From the Latrobe Survey. *(Courtesy of Delaware Public Archives)*

On the Green looking west.

struction of the Read, Jr., mansion and the Thomas hotel/residence, both on The Strand, at about the same time. The Wiley house shares design characteristics with both of those structures, as it does with the Alexander double house and the Academy. All of those buildings feature a high quality of exterior woodworking with fine punch-and-gouge detailing. Yet while similarities can easily lead observers to see the fine hand of Crouding, to date no documentary evidence exists to prove that link. The Wiley house needs no extra attributions, for the quality of the structure speaks for itself, from its proportions to its exterior ornamentation, particularly the door surround and cornice, both elaborate, yet controlled. The house at Number 8, built shortly before the Wiley house, provides a good stylistic comparison, as does the slightly later house at Number 24. Number 8 was constructed by 1788 and expanded between 1794 and 1797. Unlike the Wiley house, this solidly built house is plain and unornamented, as is the frame house at Number 24, with its front section dating to about 1815.

Two other handsome brick residences, both built before the economic downturn of the 1840s, exemplify the mature Federal style in New

Watercolor by Alice Hay of East Third Street facing the Green. *(Courtesy of New Castle Historical Society)*

Castle. They are Number 16, the Rodney house, and Number 46, Harmony house. Those houses share a number of design characteristics such as door surrounds, corbelled cornices, and decorative stone lintels. The building at Number 16 has an adjoining wing that was originally a law office. Both of those houses have passed down in the same families for a hundred and fifty or more years, a tradition of continuity unusual on this street or anywhere else in town.

Sometimes facades do not tell the whole story. Number 12 began as a two-story house in the 1820s, but a third story was added in the next decade. With its shallowly pitched roof and corbelled brick cornice the house projects a Greek Revival look, which was subsequently enhanced when a Greek Revival porch was added about 1900.

Three more buildings on the block illustrate late-nineteenth-century styles ranging from vernacular to professionally designed, from functional to ornate. There is a frame dwelling with bracketed cornice at Number 20 and an unusual gable-end frame house at Number 10 that features a two-story bay window, diamond-shaped wood shingles, and a porch replete with jigsaw trim. These buildings appear to share nothing in common with each other or with their neighbors along

John Wiley built the house at 18 East Third Street in 1801.

Doorway of 18 East Third Street displays elaborate woodworking.

46 East Third Street.

12-16 East Third Street.

8-12 East Third Street.

the block, but when you stand on the Green and look at the ensemble of structures, you notice not their random order by date of construction or style, but the harmonious interaction of well-cared for buildings.

East Fourth Street from Delaware Street to Harmony Street

Fourth Street dates back in time, if not in name, to the earliest years of Dutch settlement. It was called the Second Row, one of the two streets that Peter Stuyvesant approved for settlement in 1655. By the time of William Penn, Fourth Street had been divided into three parcels that were subsequently subdivided into building lots. Fragmentary evidence suggests that this first block of Fourth Street, between Delaware Street and Harmony Street, has remained true to its heritage as Dutch Second Row. It developed more slowly than did its neighboring blocks closer to the river and became a place favored by artisans and shopkeepers who served the local community.

The oldest remaining house on the block is the Amstel House, the impres-

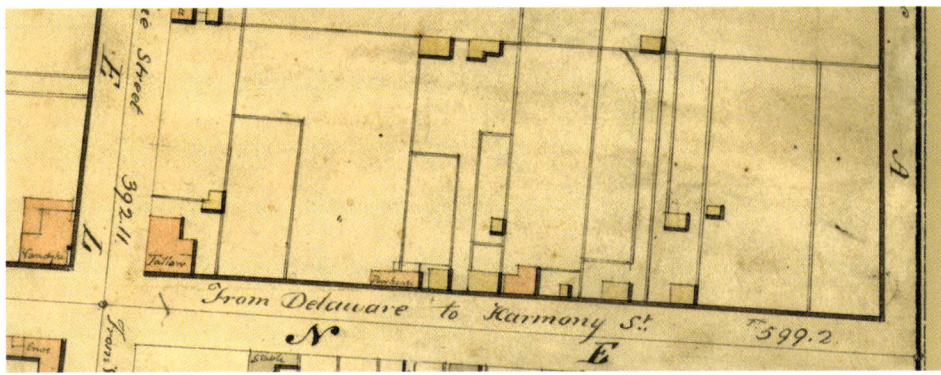

East Fourth Street from Delaware Street to Harmony Street in 1804-1805. From the Latrobe Survey. *(Courtesy of Delaware Public Archives)*

sive high-style Georgian structure at 2 East Fourth described in the Architecture section, which was built in the 1730s to replace a yet earlier structure. Several other houses on the block date to circa 1800 and can be seen on the Latrobe plan of 1805. Latrobe

18-24 East Fourth Street shows the evolution of styles over the centuries.

shows a building in the middle of the block that he designated as a poorhouse. Here is an unusual, if not unique, example of early private charity in the community. In his will, one citizen left his house to be used by the town for the care of those without resources, a generous act in an age before publicly

16-20 East Fourth Street.

built facilities existed for the homeless poor, the old, and the incapacitated in Delaware. How the poorhouse worked we do not know, but at least we

23-25 East Fourth Street.

know that it existed, thanks to the Latrobe survey. Some portions of the poorhouse building still exist, incorporated into Number 18, as can be seen in that building's brickwork. Note particularly the irregular sections of eighteenth-century glazed-header Flemish bond bricks.

Fourth Street developed slowly in the decades following Latrobe's mapping. Some buildings on the block date to the 1830s and 1840s, particularly the vernacular Greek Revival row of brick townhouses at numbers 10 through 16. The majority of the buildings, however, date from between about 1880 to 1900 and present mostly frame examples of vernacular Italianate expression. Indeed, all of the buildings on the south side of the block date from the late nineteenth and early twentieth centuries except the mid-nineteenth-century frame house at Number 39. That house was moved to East Fourth Street in 1938 from its original location on East Third Street to allow for the creation of a garden at the Dutch House. Numbers 41-43 and 51-53 are all twentieth century. The latter is an adaptive use of a large garage.

Today the first block of Fourth Street east of Delaware street is fully residential, but that has not always been the case. Even the venerable Amstel House was for a time used commercially as home to a tailor and a barber shop, and Number 38 was once a neighborhood grocery store.

THE EAST SIDE

Early Development

For its first quarter century or so after 1651, the town centered on the area from Fort Casimir, located near the marshland above the intersection of today's Second and Chestnut streets, to the Market Plaine, today's Green. The first wind-powered gristmill, and probably also a brick kiln and a brewery lay on the northeastern marshy edges of the area, while the leading Dutch administrators claimed most of the land along Harmony Street from river's edge to Third Street for their houses, large gardens, and orchards.

In subsequent decades under the planning of William Penn's government, the town's center moved beyond Harmony to Delaware Street, and the old center effectively became the east side of New Castle's historic area. No remnants of the fort or of the earliest period of settlement have survived. Only the marshes still exist, although now greatly reduced in size, and highways now define the shape of the area inland from the river.

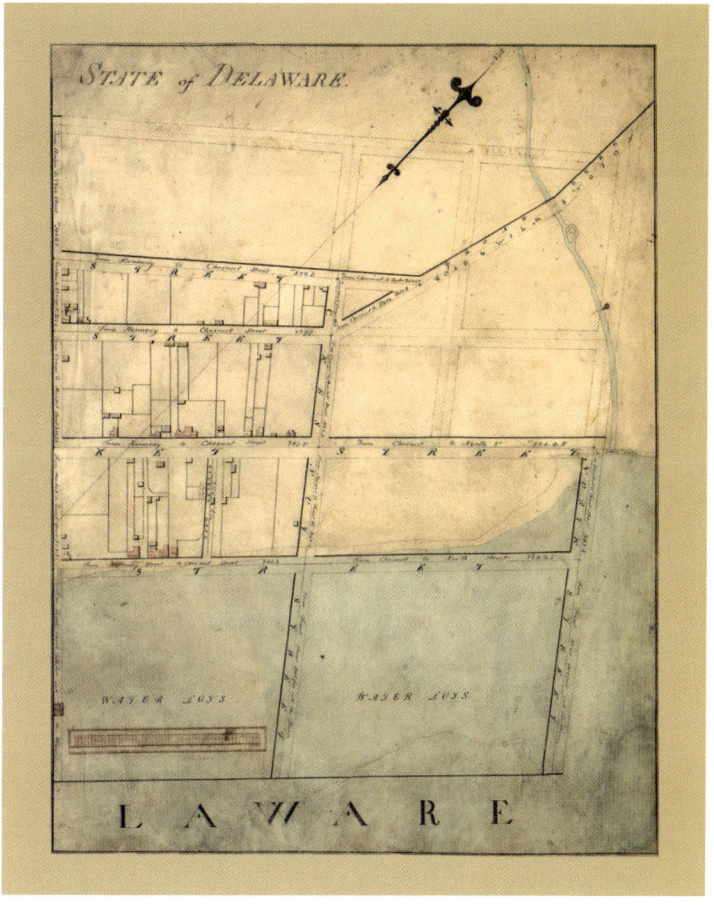

East of the Green as delineated by the Latrobe Survey of 1804-05. *(Courtesy of Delaware Public Archives)*

There are no visible remains of the bustle that once took place along the riverfront on the Harmony Street wharf, the town's earliest wharf. Today the east side is nineteenth century in its architectural styles and residential in character.

To stand at the river end of Harmony Street and look downriver is to see landscaped grounds that began to take shape in the 1920s, as a yacht basin, a tennis court, and ornamental gardens replaced warehouses and other outbuildings. Gone forever were the commercial, industrial, and passenger wharfs of the nineteenth century and before.

The foot of Harmony Street itself was once a center of economic activity. It provided the site for the town's first public wharf as well as a passenger wharf for cross-Delaware ferry traffic begun in 1724. Now only three buildings still

Looking from the Delaware River to Harmony Street wharf and east side of New Castle in the late nineteenth century. *(Courtesy of New Castle Historical Society)*

stand as silent reminders of the noise, bustle, and necessary accommodations of what was once a busy port and commercial area. The hotel and house at 100 Harmony Street still stands, but it has been greatly expanded to provide classroom and office space for Immanuel Church. Two smaller, less architec-

turally detailed buildings of the colonial and Federal periods that provided refreshment and even accommodation also remain at 118 Harmony and 114 East Second Street. The oldest part of the building at 114 Second dates to about 1750. Best known as the Spread Eagle Tavern, it has been expanded over time for use as an hotel and now a residence, but the brickwork on the south-

114 East Second Street under restoration in 2011. The first section dates to about 1750 when it was the Spread Eagle Tavern.

Detail of side wall of the oldest section of 114 East Second Street, where brickwork shows the many changes that have occurred to the building over more than 250 years.

west side of the building reveals its age and the changes it has undergone. The Harmony Street property, known as the Rising Sun Tavern, was built in 1796, with an addition in 1801. In its early years as a tavern, the front room served the public; private groups met in the back room; a window on the river side provided take-away service; and the cook worked in the basement. A mid-nineteenth-century frame addition was demolished in the 1940s. Its removal left an unusually shaped roofline for a building that is now a residence.

Three other late-eighteenth-century buildings can be seen just above the old tavern at 122, 124, and 126 Harmony. William Armstrong, himself a tavern keeper on The Strand and a developer, built all three attached structures. Their solid but plain facades suggest he built them for tradesmen or skilled artisans. Other late-eighteenth-century buildings on Second Street also provided sturdy, unadorned houses for skilled and unskilled workers. Of particular interest is the frame double house at 156 and 158, built by John Aull about 1797. Those houses predate the row of three houses he built down the block closer to the market that are known familiarly as Aull's Row.

The early-nineteenth-century Latrobe map shows a scattering of buildings on Second, Third, and Fourth streets between Harmony and Chestnut. One of those buildings, still standing at 159 East Third, would then have been at the edge of the town. The two-story, two-bay build-

Built as the Rising Sun Tavern in 1796, this building at 118 Harmony Street is now a residence.

Compare this double house built by John Aull about 1797 at 156-158 Second Street with the row of three houses he built about 1801 at 47-51 East Second Street and his higher-style double house at 53-55 The Strand.

ing is sturdy but plain. Its only decoration comes from the yellow brick relieving arches over the windows that offer a counterpoint to the red brick of the walls.

An east-side location away from the bustle of downtown New Castle must have appealed to Thomas Clayton and his son-in-law Nathaniel Young, for the two men and Young's two daughters, built a fine Federal-style house at 144 East Third Street in about 1830. Unlike similar sized houses in the town's center, this house stands back from the street within a large piece of property able to support gardens and outbuildings. The house displays understated ornamentation of the late Federal style with a fan-lighted doorway, corbelled cornice, and parapet chimney. Perhaps the almost rural setting appealed to two wealthy transplants from Kent and Sussex counties. Clayton, a United States Representative and then Senator, Secretary of State of Delaware, and Chief Justice of Delaware came to New Castle at the end of his career. Young, a retired military officer, became a major general of the Delaware militia and a businessman of considerable wealth. By the end of the century, when Young's daughters still lived in the house, East Third was no longer the edge of town. Houses now lined both sides of the street.

The population of the town of New Castle dropped so precipitously between 1840 and 1850 that it took three decades for the town to recover.

159 East Third Street.

By 1880 the "new" New Castle had added industrial activities. The factories and mills needed workers, both skilled and unskilled, and the workers needed places to live. From its nadir of about 1200 people in 1850, the town more than doubled by 1880. That growth spurred the largest building boom within the town's historic core and transformed both the east and west sides of New Castle. Existing houses were often expanded or replaced; empty lots were built upon; and whole new areas opened to settlement. Streets plotted on the Latrobe survey finally came into being, and still more streets were needed.

114 East Third Street, built about 1830 on a site then at the edge of town.

100 block of East Third Street captures a wide range of vernacular examples of architectural styles.

Building Out the East Side

Today the east side of New Castle contains more than two hundred structures, about 70 percent built in the nineteenth century, and the majority of those late in that century. With only a few exceptions, most noted in the previous section on architectural styles, the housing of the east side of New Castle reflects vernacular craftsmanship. Builders combined elements of various currently fashionable architectural styles freely, so houses have roofs of pitches ranging from steep to almost flat, some with dormers and some without. Most facades lack ornamentation beyond perhaps a rectangular- or fan-shaped piece of glass above the front door. Cornices range

200 block of East Fourth Street.

from corbelled brick to plain boxed to heavy brackets in a variety of designs. Some houses seem to reflect Greek Revival influence, particularly those built before the Civil War. Houses built after the war are most likely to be Italianate in style—but not always. That is why it is so enjoyable to walk through the neighborhood to discover interesting and sometimes surprising style combinations or juxtapositions.

The house at 409 Harmony Street is an example of a building that defies style categorization. Here is a mid-nineteenth-century brick house with gable roof, fanlight over door, and bracketed cornice. Like the Dutch House of a much earlier period, it is vernacular to the core. Owner changes over time provide an additional challenge for those on an architectural style stroll. Take, for example, 226 and 228 East Second Street. Here are two sides of a double house, built in the 1890s, that share a bracketed cornice and have the same window lintels but no longer have a common roofline or similar style of door surround.

Over the course of the nineteenth century, rows of houses grew in length from doubles, like those at 127 and 129 Harmony, built circa 1844, to a row of nine that face the Green and dominate the 200 block of Harmony Street. The structure at numbers 127-129 is a straightforward gable-roofed frame building constructed as two two-bay units, with central chimney, single dormers, and transoms above the doors. The row of nine in the next block (numbers

127-129 Harmony Street, built about 1844.

203-19) dates about
fifty years later. They
are shallow-roofed,
three-bay-wide, brick
structures that share
a bracketed cornice.
The corner house
was built as a sepa-
rate, larger unit but
connects at cornice
level with the long

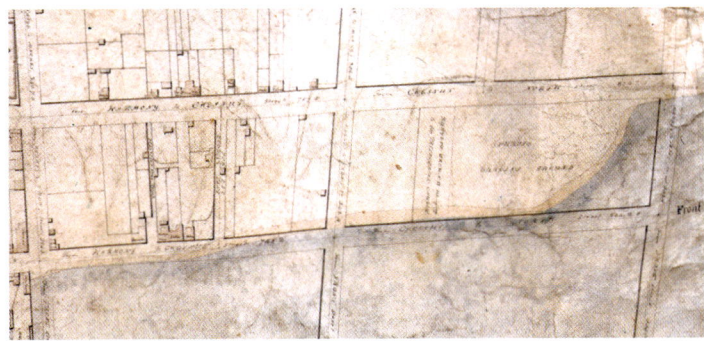

A Potter's Field and a cemetery for the Presbyterian Church were
located in the area of East Second Street beyond Chestnut Street.
This area, now called Bull Hill, began to be developed in the
1880s. From an uncolored private copy of the Latrobe Survey.
(Courtesy of New Castle Historical Society)

row. Another interesting late-nineteenth-century row of workers' houses can
be found at 207-17 East Second, the vicinity of the town's original fort. Interestingly, each house increases slightly in width with the largest located at
the corner of Second and Chestnut. When built, every house had two rooms
on two floors, but over time owners have expanded them to take advantage
of unobstructed river views.

After Fort Casimir disappeared, its immediate surrounding area did not
remain unused, for a cemetery plot or Potter's Field was set aside for use
as the town's free burying ground for the indigent or the incarcerated. By
the middle of the nineteenth century, though, this area began to experience development pressures. Initially, people sought the sand of the area to
use elsewhere, which exposed graves. Then by the 1880s the land itself had
grown in value, and houses and outbuildings had started to appear. Today
that area, often called Bull Hill, contains houses that range in date from
1880 to the present. There is also a small park, a boat club, and the last
building in town before the Foot Dyke, a modern building with a bas-relief
medallion of an historic schooner on its front façade that is part of the town's
water facilities.

Whatever their pitch of roof or level of exterior ornamentation, most of
the houses built on the east side of New Castle in the nineteenth century
reflected local builders' interpretations of the prevailing regional style of
townhouses. It was a style that retained the box-like shape of the Georgian

Double house with mansard roof at 122-124 East Third Street.

The early-twentieth-century bungalow at 182 East Fourth Street probably came from the Sears Roebuck Company.

and Federal periods. Yet the east side also contains vernacular examples of the various styles that captivated late-nineteenth- and early-twentieth-century America. An example of a Second Empire mansard roof can be found at 122-124 East Third, and a Queen Anne-influenced house replete with large front porch and a mix of brick and wooden siding stands at 182 East Fourth. Early-twentieth-century bungalow examples can be found on East Second, Third, and Fourth streets, including the house at 184 East Fourth. This small, one-story-with-attic frame house has a hipped roof and exposed rafters. Good examples of house styles of the 1900-15 period with front gables and cross gables, pent eaves, and fish scales can be found at 141, 143, and 145 East Second Street. Unique for the east side of town is 166 East Second, a purpose-built apartment house dating to about 1910.

As the large number of modern, or post-1950, houses located in the Bull Hill area attest, development and redevelopment of New Castle's east side has been on-going. Fully 30 percent of the houses there date from 1950 to the present. Some are in discernable "modern" styles of post-World War II America; some are in Colonial Revival styles that suggest but do not duplicate the past; and some, particularly those built most recently, strive to look as much as possible like early Georgian or Federal townhouses.

Census records and other sources add considerable information on the people who lived in the houses of New Castle's east side in the mid to late nineteenth century. By occupation, most were considered unskilled workers. For those with skills, the range of occupations was very large. There were east siders

141-145 East Second Street.

who made or repaired clothes or shoes, baked bread, or butchered and sold meat; others worked in the building trades or in every type of transportation from boat to horse to railroad. There were teachers, firemen, printers, and even the town crier. Many worked in the town's factories in a variety of skilled or semi-skilled trades. Keepers of hotels and saloons lived and worked on the east side, as did retired people, widows, and people with no recorded information.

Among the few inhabitants of the east side who were high-income individuals, two earned their wealth through their skills as a machinist and as a cabinetmaker. The daughters of Nathanial Young were unusual residents of the neighborhood, for they lived on inherited wealth in the family house at 144 East Third through the nineteenth century.

The mingling of occupations and wealth mirrored the mixing of ethnicities and races. Every street had whites and African Americans, native-born and foreign-born. Those with the fewest economic resources tended to live farthest away from the town's center, moving into the area of Third and Fourth streets closest to Chestnut and to the marshier areas. On Fourth Street in the 1870s, for example, African Americans and Irish predominated, often living side by side.

The Irish were the first immigrant group to settle in New Castle in large numbers in the nineteenth century. After the calamitous potato famine of 1848, a trickle became a stream. In 1850 nearly 7 percent of New Castle's

The congregation of Mount Salem Methodist Episcopal Church, 140 East Fourth Street, replaced their original frame church with this handsome brick structure in the late 1870s.

residents had been born in Ireland, a percentage that had risen to almost 11 percent twenty years later. Irish immigrants lived on the east and west sides of town, but their church and later a parochial school rose on the east side at Fifth and Harmony streets. Most of the Irish arrived as unskilled laborers, but by 1870 Irish men could be found in most occupations, including politics and what we would today call the hospitality industry, such as saloon-keeping and inn-keeping. Irish females who worked are identified as servants or domestics, including no doubt washerwomen. Some lived in the houses of their employers, but many lived in their own homes.

The African-American population of New Castle increased in number but declined as a percentage of population between 1830 and 1870. In that latter year about 19 percent of the townspeople were African American. African Americans faced the most limited employment options. Even after the abolition of slavery, only a few individuals could climb beyond laborer or servant. Two of the more successful African Americans lived on East Fourth Street in 1870. One listed his occupation as gardener and the other as hackman and both had wealth levels comparable to their Irish-born neighbor, the town crier. African-American working women, like their Irish counterparts, usually were servants or domestics. Interestingly, in the 1860 census, most African Americans in service were designated as *servants,* while whites, usually from Ireland or England, were listed as *domestics,* a distinction that disappeared in the subsequent census.

One impetus to African-American settlement in the area of East Fourth Street between Harmony and Chestnut streets was the organization of Mount

Salem Methodist Episcopal Church in the 1840s. By 1878 the congregation had outgrown its original frame church and replaced it with a modest yet handsome brick structure in the Gothic Revival style. Pointed windows topped by pointed arches framed within vertically pointed recessed wall sections work together in the same spirit as the greatest Gothic cathedral to draw the eye heavenward. Mount Salem has served its congregation for over a century.

In addition to Mount Salem Methodist Episcopal Church and Saint Peter's Roman Catholic Church, a Baptist church once stood on the east side at Fifth and Cherry streets, an area that was just beginning to develop in the early 1870s. Two real-estate agents sold the congregation land in 1872-73, and by the time the church was completed in 1879, only one or two other buildings shared the area. Like Mount Salem, First Baptist was a Gothic Revival style brick church. A steeply roofed cupola carried the sense of verticality upward from the equally steeply sloped portico. Initially the church struggled. Its first minister came only once a week—by fishing boat from New Jersey—but ninety years later, in the 1960s, a growing congregation decided to move to open space just out of town, where they built a large complex of church, school, and meeting space. The site of the original church is now a parking lot behind the post office.

The final expansion of the east side saw the development of Fifth and Sixth streets as well as a new cross street, Cherry Street, an area that today lies beyond the border of the town's historic core. The housing in this area, as well as on the eastern edges of Third

Cars and ferries brought great activity to Chestnut Street from 1926 to 1951. Ferries provided the only direct connection between Delaware and New Jersey until the Delaware Memorial Bridge opened in 1951. *(Courtesy of New Castle Historical Society)*

Ferry entrance as it looked in the 1930s. *(Courtesy of New Castle Historical Society)*

and Fourth streets, provide visual examples of many of the style options for the late nineteenth and twentieth centuries. Particularly of note is the row of ten connected brick houses on Cherry Street. Built in the late nineteenth century with flat roofs, fan lights over the front doors, and a continuous bracketed cornice, these houses provided needed living space for workers in New Castle's still-expanding industries.

The confluences of marshy land and the need to facilitate traffic using the New Jersey-Delaware ferry led to the construction of what is called the Ferry

Aerial view of New Castle after the construction of the Ferry Cut-Off. *(Courtesy of New Castle Historical Society)*

Cut-Off, a curved section of road designed to connect the wharf at the end of Chestnut Street directly with Basin Road. The cut-off precluded additional contiguous residential growth in the town's northeastern sector, but it routed automobile traffic to the terminal with a minimum of impact on the rest of New Castle. This was especially important on summer weekends when beach traffic was at its height.

Shop windows at 111 East Third Street.

King's Ice House on Harmony Street near The Strand, now gone. *(Courtesy of Francis Pollard)*

The ferry wharf at Chestnut Street marked the last commercial use of the town's river front and the last major commercial activity on the east side. The small businesses such as corner grocery stores or tailor shops that had dotted the east side are now gone, but their locations can often still be seen in the corner-cut doorways and plate-glass display windows. Gone too are commercial sites, such as the old ice company that was once located on Harmony between the Strand and Second streets and the steel mill on the river north of the town's center.

THE WEST SIDE

Shaped by Industry

The New Castle & Frenchtown Railroad Company's tiny wooden ticket office standing near the entrance to Battery Park at the foot of Delaware Street offers a good place to begin to comprehend the evo-

First ticket office for the New Castle and Frenchtown Railroad, second oldest such building in the United States. It barely escaped destruction before its restoration in the 1950s.

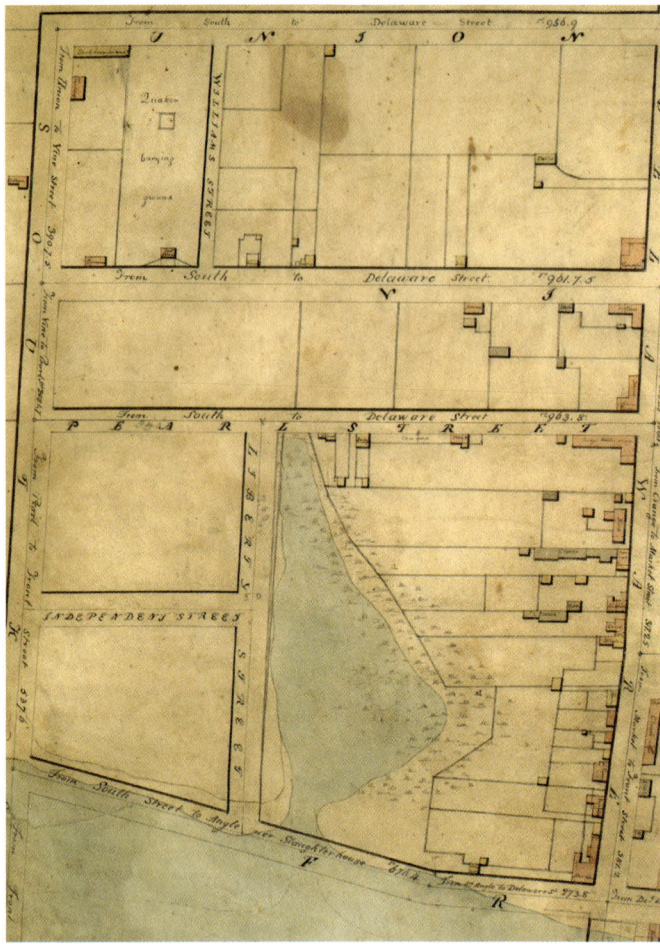

West side of New Castle from Delaware Street to South Street and the river to Fourth Street. From the Latrobe Survey. *(Courtesy of Delaware Public Archives)*

lution of New Castle's west side. The ticket office that looks so quaint and unobtrusive in the park today was in reality the harbinger of extensive transportation and industrial developments that propelled New Castle's economy from the 1830s into the twentieth century. Ironically, for all their once-great power, the railroads' physical presence is now largely gone, but they shaped the west side of town.

The railroads accelerated a pattern of land use that dated back to the town's early days. Latrobe's town plan of 1805 shows little settlement west of Delaware Street, just a handful of houses plus a slaughterhouse near the river by the marsh, a cow yard, a bark house and tannery, and several stables. All of those businesses were important but highly odiferous, best suited to the town's periphery.

The New Castle and Frenchtown Railroad was built to connect the Delaware River to the Chesapeake Bay in the 1830s, during the earliest days of railroad construction in the United States. It was constructed through undeveloped land west of town to meet the river near Delaware Street adjacent to an area where former marshland and a slough had only recently been drained.

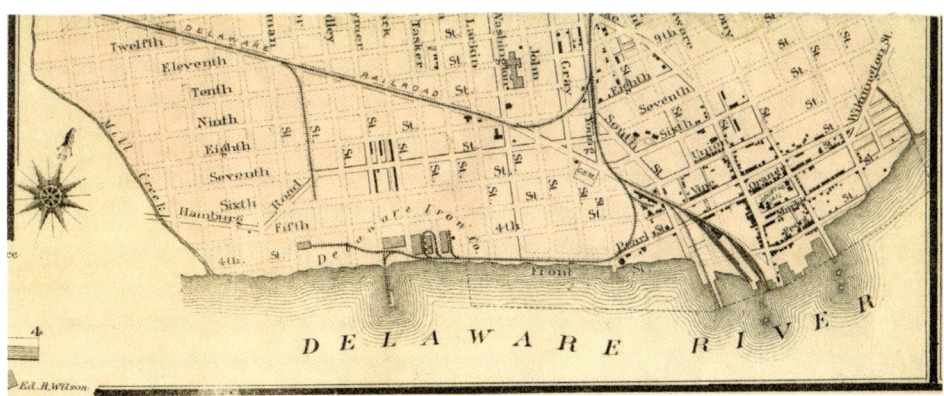

Detail from Hopkins' *New Castle County Atlas* of 1881. *(Courtesy of Delaware Historical Society)*

The railroad began as a single line with a passenger and freight depot in what is now the heart of Battery Park. The tracks connected to a wharf, which was built at the foot of Delaware Street with earth removed in the regrading process required to build the railroad. Over time the area became a railroad yard, with six other tracks that reached down to the riverside from the main railroad line like fingers on a hand.

The New Castle & Frenchtown Railroad was sold to its much larger rival, the Philadelphia, Wilmington & Baltimore Railroad, in 1839. Some years later the Philadelphia, Wilmington & Baltimore realigned the original NC&FT tracks to unite with new track it laid south from Wilmington. The two lines met near the intersection of Ninth and Tenth streets with Young Street. The major casualty of the realignment was the Presbyterian Church because the NC&FT Railroad pro-vided the only access to their cem-etery just west of town. Fortunately, the PW&B Railroad solved the problem by building a road to re-place the old tracks. Later still, the PW&B was absorbed into the na-tion's largest rail system, that of the Pennsylvania Railroad. New Castle was thus connected to the main rail

Late-nineteenth-century group picture of work-ers at the Tasker plant. *(Courtesy of New Castle Historical Society)*

Employees at the Deemer Steel plant pose, early twentieth century. *(Courtesy of New Castle Historical Society)*

lines of the eastern United States, and the town's leaders were eager to give permission to extend tracks and sidings and to allow new or extended wharfs to assist enterprises that were willing to establish factories there.

The first entrepreneurs to seize upon the opportunity that the railroad represented were several local men who in 1833 incorporated as the New Castle Manufacturing Company. Located adjacent to the railroad line near the intersection of as yet undeveloped land in the vicinity of Fifth and South streets, the company commenced building railroad locomotives, first for the NC&FT, then later for other railroads. The manufacturing property had an interesting history. For a decade or so the local company was successful in an increasingly competitive market until they sold their business to another steam-engine producer who in turn sold the factory to Philadelphian Thomas Tasker. Tasker, whose multi-pronged role in New Castle's development is discussed in the History section, turned the property into a steam-powered flour mill. He later sold it to Thomas Lea and Sons, millers of Wilmington, who subsequently relocated their flour milling operations farther west near Seventh and Washington streets. The flour mill operated there until 1900. The old foundry passed into new hands and was abandoned by the early 1890s.

In 1872 when Tasker sold his flour mill, he created the Delaware Iron Company on an extensive piece of property west of Washington Street at the river. The plant had its own railroad spur line that ran along what is now the waterfront walk to the end of the company's wharf. Tasker's iron factory manufactured gas and water pipes and by 1875 employed 350 hands.

Other large industrial plants were also constructed along railroad sidings on New Castle's west side. In 1860 James G. Shaw of Chester, Pennsylvania, built a large cotton mill at Ninth and Washington streets called the Triton

Cotton Mill. At its height in the late nineteenth century, Triton Cotton Mill employed over 125 workers to convert raw cotton into thread. Shaw originally had a partner named James G. Knowles, but they had a falling out. In 1878 Knowles opened a woolen mill located a few blocks away along the rail-

Plate in *Atlas of New Castle County* (Philadelphia: G. W. Baist, 1893). *(Courtesy of University of Delaware Library, Newark, Del.)*

Coal yards once stood in what is now Battery Park. The building on the right, 1 The Strand, was once owned by the New Castle & Frenchtown Railroad and has been expanded to be a private residence. *(Courtesy of New Castle Historical Society)*

road line at Washington Street between Seventh and Eighth streets. The Knowles mill employed as many as 200 hands. Knowles' mill, like its near neighbor, the flour mill, closed in 1900, victims of larger, more modern national brands that could underprice them.

The Triton Cotton Mill also closed, but that property was bought by iron maker Selden Deemer, who established the Deemer Steel Company on the site. That casting plant continued to operate until the late twentieth century.

All of New Castle's industries, as well at its households, needed coal to fuel the engines and furnaces that powered equipment and heated spaces. Some businessmen thought New Castle would also make a good port for the exporting of coal from the mines of Pennsylvania. In 1863 a group of investors built a long wharf, elevated some twenty feet in the air, adjacent to South Street. Their plan was to run a railroad spur line down from the main line all the way out to the end of the wharf. There cars loaded with coal could dump their loads down into the holds of ships below. Unfortunately, the men's engineering skills proved better than their business plan. Within a few years the business ceased, and the wharf lay abandoned. A more successful coal transfer venture flourished on the railroad company's original property at Delaware Street and the river.

Those industries, plus the even larger steel-casting plants being built along the Delaware River, set the tone for the development of a housing market on the west side of New Castle. The area became the home for industrial employees from top management to the workers.

Patterns of Development

The patterns of development of New Castle's east and west sides differ significantly. On the east side topography and roads created one finite space for contiguous development. The west side offered more space, but the location of railroad lines and factories divided that space into sections. On the west side, development took place both northeast and southwest of the Pennsylvania Railroad's two lines into New Castle as well as northwest and southeast of the old PW&B line. Most of the rails are now gone, but the divisions of development in the nineteenth and twentieth centuries remain. The Latrobe plan of gridded streets can be seen from the river to Sixth Street between Delaware and South streets, but even the great Latrobe could not have planned for the placement of Allen Lesley's estate nor of the railroads and the highways that have imposed their will on the west side's development.

From the River to Fifth Street

The area from the river west of Delaware Street to Fifth Street is today included in New Castle's historic district. Development there was slow into the early nineteenth century. The oldest house still standing, 25 West Fourth Street, dates from about 1800 and sits in splendid isolation in the Latrobe survey. As the block filled in, the old house became a combination grocery and bakery for the neighborhood. Today it is again a residence, one of few survivors among pre-Civil War buildings on the west side.

In the first half of the nineteenth century, houses, warehouses, and other outbuildings began to rise on the blocks west of the town's his-

25 West Fourth Street.

15 and 17 West Fourth Street at Delaware Street.

toric center, but few have survived. Those that remain reveal vernacular style patterns similar to those of the more rapidly developing east side. Most are attached dwellings. All have gable roofs and are two or two-and-a-half stories tall and two or three bays in width. Some have been altered over time, but good examples can still be found, including the row of four brick houses at 26-32 West Fourth Street, which exemplify New Castle's Greek Revival style with small upper windows and plain transoms above their front doors.

Moving up both sides of West Fourth Street toward Delaware Street are seven brick houses, attached and detached, that showcase the glories of the highly ornamental styles of the late nineteenth century. In the brief period from about 1878 to 1885 these houses were built with Italianate, Gothic Revival and Second Empire features for downtown merchants or skilled craftsmen. These original owners were not trained in the professions nor were they industrialists. They did not come from backgrounds of privilege. They were solid, successful middle-class businessmen. The double house at numbers 22-24 is the only one designed by an architect for his client, the bricklayer Aquila Hizar. All of the houses on this block showcase the types of wooden ornamentation made possible by mass production. There are bargeboards, scrolled cornice brackets with or without ornamented friezes, and varieties of elaborate turned or cut woodwork. There are also examples of decorative stone lintels and brickwork, bay windows, and other irregularities designed to break up the surface of a building. Interesting

15 West Fourth Street.   and unusual for the time and location are the

slight set-backs for all but one of the houses. For comparison's sake, note numbers 13 and 15 on West Third Street. Here are smaller, less exuberant expressions of late-nineteenth-century housing. This brick pair dates from about 1880 and has impressive black and tan decorative brickwork and colorful pressed-tin cornices.

17 West Fourth Street.

The most stylish houses on West Third and Fourth streets were built closest to Delaware Street. This was an area where shopkeepers and master craftsmen lived. The further one moves southwest down those blocks, the more the houses become smaller in size and plainer in design. Workers, mostly unskilled, lived on that end of the blocks.

A row of ten houses (numbers 34-52) can be found on West Fourth Street below Foundry Street. They were built at the end of the Civil War and designated "negro tenements" on a late-nineteenth-century insurance survey. By the time of the

114-116 West Fourth Street.

Civil War, African Americans lived on both sides of New Castle, usually in the same less expensive areas affordable to laborers of all ethnicities and races. That particular section along West Fourth Street, however, appears to have contained a concentration of African Americans because of the proximity of an African-American church and school on Williams Street. But not all of the inhabitants of lower West Fourth Street were African Americans. Well into the twentieth century, immigrants, particularly Irish, and native-born whites shared the neighborhood.

West Fourth Street near South Street, 1942. *(Courtesy of New Castle Historical Society)*

Williams Street runs for only one block between Fourth and Fifth streets, yet this one block's history tells a great deal about African-American life in nineteenth- and early-twentieth-century New Castle. Two major institutions of the town's black community, a church and a school, made the block a center for African-American life.

Union African Methodist Church, originally called Bethany Church, faces Williams Street at the corner of Fifth Street. A cemetery surrounds the church. The present plain brick church, now covered with stucco, was built in 1863 to replace an earlier frame church of 1818. The building has been rebuilt twice: in 1888 and 1927. This church is home to the oldest African-American congregation in New Castle. Its origins date to 1817, when a group of African Americans in New Castle joined the movement begun by Peter Spencer in Wilmington four years earlier to create an independent African-American Methodist church separate from the control of white religious leaders. Spencer's African Methodist movement gained adherents throughout Delaware and in other nearby states. By the time of Spencer's death in 1843,

Union African Methodist Church at the corner of West Fifth Street and Williams Street. Originally called Bethany Church, it is the oldest African-American congregation in New Castle.

thirty-one congregations were affiliated with the conference, which continues to recall its founding at the Big Quarterly celebration held in Wilmington each August.

In mid-block on the western side of Williams Street once stood a schoolhouse whose history offers another view of the rise of the black community in the era of segregation. The Williams School was built in 1867. At that time Delaware's public schools were for whites only, but the passage of the post-Civil War Thirteenth, Fourteenth, and Fifteenth amendments to the United States Constitution promised more equal treatment

Booker T. Washington School dates to 1923. It is now part of the New Castle Community Center.

for African Americans. Those new legal freedoms energized both black and white reformers. The Freedmen's Bureau of the federal government supplied some funding to assist African Americans to build schools in former slave states, including Delaware. Additional funding came from a volunteer group called the Delaware Association for the Moral Improvement and Education of Colored People. Businessman Thomas Tasker and Dr. Allen Lesley, among other leaders in New Castle, gave the extra money needed to buy the lot, build the school, and pay a teacher. The result was that in October 1867 New Castle's African-American children had their first opportunity to attend school.

When the Freedmen's Bureau and the association of do-good helpers faded away, the State of Delaware moved slowly to continue support for the fledgling public schools for black youngsters. In 1875 the legislature adopted a law to tax black landowners to pay for black children's education. That feeble effort of state support for the segregated schools took a big step forward in 1919, when Du Pont Company president Pierre S. du Pont made a commitment to remake public education throughout Delaware for children of both races. Du Pont did not tamper with segregation, but he

Porches on West Fifth Street.

32 West Fifth Street.

did supply the funding to build schools. In New Castle his gift made possible the construction of two schools for African-American children: Buttonwood School on Route 9 and Booker T. Washington School on South Street, which replaced the Williams Street School in 1923. Desegregation in the 1950s put an end to the all-black Booker T. Washington School, but the building continues to serve the whole community as the core of the New Castle Senior Center.

The earliest development along West Fifth Street did not begin until the middle of the nineteenth century, and it took several more decades for the block to fill in. Today the street displays a wide range of styles of houses built from about 1880 to 1930. Houses on the south side of West Fifth Street conform to the prevailing style in New Castle of the time: flat or gable roofs with bracketed cornice in single or double forms. The block provides a good range of front-porch styles that use design elements drawn from antiquity to the Gilded Age, particularly the wooden cutwork of spindle frieze, brackets, and pendant at Number 57, square columns at numbers 65 through 71, and Doric columns at numbers 73 and 75.

The opposite side of West Fifth Street has a more eclectic feel, starting with buildings that have had multiple uses over time.

120 West Fifth Street.

Of those, Number 32 has the most unusual history. That frame building began its existence as a warehouse at the South Street wharf and was moved to its present location in about 1880 to become a grocery store. It is now a residence. Next door at Number 34 is a building that began as a one-story garage in about 1916 and is now a two-story apartment building.

Just below Tremont Street three bungalows of the early 1920s capture the range of styles of the new small-house architectural trend that was sweeping across America. These three are larger than other examples of similar houses built on the east side of town. Each is a unique presentation of typical bungalow elements from overhanging eaves, exposed rafters, oversized dormers, and porches. Numbers 114 and

West Fifth Street at South Street in the 1930s. *(Courtesy of Delaware Historical Society)*

116 continue the twentieth century on West Fifth Street. Here is a frame cross-gable double house built in 1924. It is two-and-a-half stories tall and six bays wide, with porches covering the off-axis doors. It is the only such building in New Castle. The end of the block features three fine houses of the 1890s, particularly the two Queen Anne vernaculars of the Eliason brothers that are described in the Architecture section.

South Street marks the western boundary of the historic west side. In this area residential, commercial, and fraternal buildings once mixed, but today there are only residences from the late nineteenth and twentieth centuries. Gone are the lodges of fraternal orders, the factory that began as the New Castle Manufacturing Company in the 1830s, the Williams Street School, and the lumberyard begun by the Eliason brothers. Now a firehouse dominates the area.

EARLY FIRE COMPANIES

In 1796 a group of New Castle's leading citizens founded the Union Fire Company, patterned on volunteer fire companies in Philadelphia. The organizers included lawyers and businessmen who had much to lose should fire break out in their homes or offices. Each man was to purchase two leather buckets that he was to bring as speedily as possible to quench fires. Some of the founders were also members of the Trustees of the Common, which came to the fire company's assistance by purchasing a fire engine in 1819.

In 1820 a younger generation of New Castle's elite created the Penn Fire Company. When the Town Hall was planned in 1823, both companies were offered space to keep their equipment. Just a year later, on April 26, 1824, a devastating fire broke out near the present Jefferson House. Members of the two fire companies, together with every other hand available, tried their best to quench the fire as it moved quickly to destroy many buildings. Chastened by the tragedy, the Penn Fire Company purchased a more powerful hand-pumped engine capable of sending a stream of water higher than the tallest building in town. They called their engine "Good Will." It was the name that would in 1907 return as the name of New Castle's present-day fire company in this much more sophisticated age of fire fighting.

The firehouse at the corner of West Fourth and South streets is the home of the Good-Will Fire Company, No. 1, New Castle's fire department. The location is well chosen to serve the city, most particularly its oldest, most historic neighborhoods. The firehouse has seven bays for the storage of its fire trucks, an ambulance, and other motorized equipment. It is connected to a two-story, hipped-roofed building with a cupola that houses the office and rooms for the firefighters. The firehouse was built in 1957-58 with a grant from the Trustees of the Common. It was designed by Albert Kruse, the restoration architect who played an important role in New Castle's Colonial Revival movement. His plan for the firehouse pays tribute to the Town Hall of 1823, another structure funded by the Trustees of the Common, which was the first home for New Castle's fire equipment.

Fire prevention and firefighting have long played a major role in New Castle, a town that has never forgotten the devastating fire of 1824. It is no exaggeration to say that the existence of many of the town's most cherished buildings is owed to the timely intervention of the firefighters. On Delaware Street alone serious fires have been quenched at the Opera House in 1908, Bridgewater's

Goodwill Fire Company at the corner of West Fourth Street and South Street.

Jewelers in the 1940s, and the David Finney Inn in 1994. The most seriously damaged historic building to rise again after its near destruction was Immanuel Episcopal Church in 1980.

During the course of the nineteenth century, volunteer fire companies arose and dissolved in New Castle as founders died, moved away, or got too old to rush to fires with bucket or ladder in hand or to man a pump to raise a stream of water. By the 1880s two fire companies had horse-drawn steam-propelled engines, relieving volunteers of the onerous work of pumping by hand. For a short time the Lenape Fire Company was located in the Red Men's Hall at Fifth and South streets. Then in 1892 it constructed New Castle's first purpose-built firehouse located between Fifth and Sixth streets at South Street, opposite the Eliason brothers' lumberyard. Neither that building, nor the Red Men's Hall, is still standing.

In 1907 the fire companies of New Castle consolidated into the present Good-Will Company, which acquired the equipment and fire hall of the Lenape Company. The Good-Will Company got its first motorized fire truck, a pumper, in 1919. That gleaming engine no longer chases fires, but it remains a favorite feature in parades. By the 1950s the company

New Castle's first purpose-built fire station was located on South Street between Fifth and Sixth streets. Although now gone, the architecture of the building, particularly its Romanesque arches, served as an inspiration for the design of the twenty-first-century addition to the library on Delaware Street. *(Courtesy of Delaware Historical Society)*

needed a larger space to hold its growing assembly of equipment, including a marine rescue boat. The location at West Fourth and South streets, only a block away, offered an excellent choice. The fire company occupies land that belonged to New Castle's short-lived Quaker Meeting in colonial times and later the Williams Street School for African-American children.

Aerial view, about 1925, of the Lesley Mansion after it had been purchased by Stanley Deemer. No longer does the house sit on the edge of the town. *(Courtesy of New Castle Historical Society)*

Beyond the Historic District

Allen Lesley picked the site for his great Gothic Revival mansion carefully, choosing an expansive tract of land on the northwestern edge of town beyond Fifth Street, an area through which the King's Highway, the first road to connect all thirteen colonies, once ran. Around that house, built in 1855 and described in the Architecture section, he created a park-like setting full of lawns, flowers, and, particularly, trees and shrubs from around the world. A trace of the old highway can still be seen there. Then development pressures brought New Castle ever closer, and the doctor's serene country location became less idyllic. First came the rerouting of the old NC&FT Railroad line, and then in 1861 the town commissioners decided to open Sixth Street from Delaware Street to South Street. In 1864, the town's commissioners further agreed to expand the town to the west to unite with former farmland where James Shaw and then Thomas Tasker had begun to develop workers' housing around their factories.

As Sixth Street began to fill, the town commissioners agreed to open Seventh Street in 1873. To create Seventh Street required the condemnation of lands that belonged to the railroad and to Dr. Lesley. Both the doctor and the railroad initially refused compensation because they thought that the street

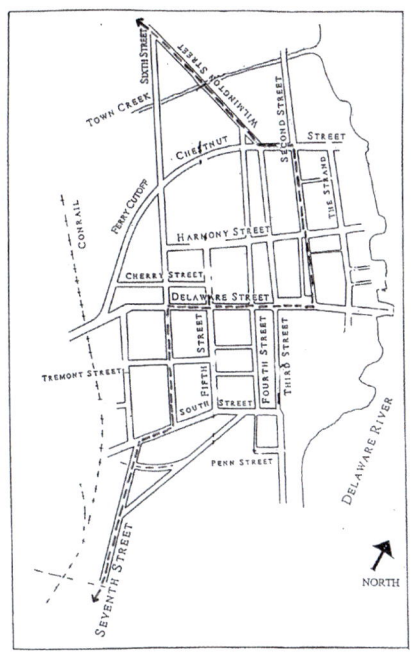

Map showing the trolley route through New Castle.

would enhance the value of their properties. When Lesley later learned the precise location of the planned street through his property, he was dismayed. Despite harsh words and threats of legal action from both the doctor and the town commissioners, the roadway went ahead. Eventually the town paid compensation to Dr. Lesley. It was a sad rupture between Lesley, then a very rich man, and the town he had loved and had served in many civic capacities, including as a town commissioner.

The die was cast in the 1860s and 1870s for expansion north and west, but, because of the location of the railroad lines, that development could not be contiguous. Sixth and Seventh streets stand on one side of a set of tracks, with Eighth Street and beyond on the other side. Sixth and Seventh streets developed very slowly, and, as they did, they followed the pattern set by the Eliason houses on West Fifth Street rather than that of the old historic core of New Castle. Lots became wider and houses began to be set back from the street. Sixth Street took on the look of a streetcar suburb, which in fact it was with the coming of the trolley in the 1890s.

It is interesting to note that the only pre-1900 house on West Sixth Street standing today is located at the western or South Street end of the block rather than at the Delaware Street end. When J. Ernest Phillips, then a young man in his early thirties, built a house at Number 111 in 1898 for himself and his

11 West Sixth Street.

wife, he clearly wanted to live close to his work in the telegraph and freight offices at Eighth and Young streets. His world was the world of the railroad and not of the old business center around the Green. Phillips's house is a large, cross-gable structure in a vernacular style that combines elements of the Queen Anne, shingle, and classical styles. Fish-scale shingles sheathe the second floor and gables, while German siding, a type of drop siding in which a concave edge at the top fits into a groove in the board above, covers the first floor. Paired pilasters and keystone-arched window frames provide classical elements in wood, as do wide and elaborately molded cornices and horizontal bands between floors. Two floors of bay windows, a two-story porch, side porch, and other overhangs create a façade that dances before your eyes. The house must have been large and expensive to maintain, for over the years the Phillips's always had boarders or extended family living with them.

Other houses on the block provide good examples of the types of Colonial Revival styles in vogue in the early twentieth century that can be found in the blocks of Sixth and Seventh streets and the block of Tremont Street that separates them. A Dutch Colonial can be found at Number 110, while Georgian-Federal-inspired Colonial Revival is at Number 107 and a large bungalow at 108. Modern styles from post-World War II into the twenty-first century, such as Cape Cods and one-floor ranch houses, can be seen on Seventh Street.

Shawtown

Shawtown is the area that remains most closely associated with the era of New Castle's industrial development in the second half of the nineteenth century. This enclave of workers' housing is essentially a triangularly shaped area. It is circumscribed by the railroad tracks between Seventh and Eighth streets

Detail from the *Baist Atlas* shows the unusual configuration of Shawtown. *(Courtesy of University of Delaware Library, Newark, Del.)*

that can be viewed as its base and goes to the apex created by the junction of the old New Castle and Frenchtown Turnpike and Washington Street. It is called Shawtown in recognition of its original developer, James G. Shaw, who created the Triton Cotton Mill. Contained as it is between railroad tracks and major highways and with acutely angled land parcels,

New Castle passenger depot, 1946. The site of the station at Young Street above Eighth is now a park. *(Courtesy of Hagley Museum and Library)*

the area became a self-contained community within a larger town.

But if the railroads and mills created Shawtown, they also divided it. There was another set of railroad tracks, now gone, that ran through the center of Shawtown along Young and South streets and then split into two sets of tracks at Ninth Street. If that sounds convoluted and confusing, it is. But stand in the triangularly shaped park that has been created on the land where all three sets of tracks once connected and look in all directions to orient yourself. The area east of the South-Young street tracks was residential, while fac-

tories and houses shared the area to the west. Major railroad facilities straddled the tracks. New Castle's rail passenger depot stood at Young Street above Eighth Street in what is now the park, and the freight office and its depot stood on the opposite side of the street and tracks above Ninth Street. Both railroad depots are now gone, but two

Tracks converging at the passenger and freight depots. *(Courtesy of Hagley Museum and Library)*

buildings that served the needs of railroad passengers and workers, including traveling businessmen, still stand. The Railroad Hotel is located on the west side of Seventh Street below Eighth Street. The two-part building is now apartments. Further along at the northwest corner of Young and Ninth streets stands the U.S. Hotel, now derelict.

The eastern side of Shawtown contained housing for those who worked in the mills as well as stores that served the community and those who were passing through on the railroad. First Shaw's cotton mill and then Deemer's steel mill that replaced it dominated the west side of Shawtown, but close behind the building of factories came workers' housing. At its height as a semi-self-contained community, Shawtown had, in addition to hotels, neighborhood shops ranging from bakeries to butcher shops and groceries, cigar stores, saloons, plus its own school and even a church.

The church was an early effort by New Castle's Episcopal congregation at Immanuel on the Green to reach out to the developing community of workers. The congregation built a small chapel and Sunday school in 1869 at the corner of Ninth and Clayton streets on land donated by James M. Johns, son of Kensey Johns, Jr. The building did not hold up well, nor did it attract a self-sustaining congregation. By the early twentieth century services had ended, and the church was torn down. Since Immanuel had not been able to buy adjacent land earlier when they had wanted to add a cemetery, the vestry of Immanuel Church sold this small parcel in 1923.

Shawtown has always been a multi-ethnic community. In the late nineteenth century native-born Americans constituted the largest share of the population, while the Irish accounted for the largest immigrant group. One such family was that of Alice Brady, a native of Ireland. In 1870 her household consisted of herself as head of house and three teenaged sons, all of whom walked from their house at Ninth and Young streets to work in the cotton mill. Two of the boys, John and James, stayed in Shawtown and became shopkeepers, selling groceries and cigars. When John died, the family had gained sufficient wealth to fund the construction of the bell tower at Saint Peter's Roman Catholic Church as his memorial. Until Alice died in 1903, she lived in Shawtown on Ninth Street.

Over the decades industrial opportunities continued to bring new groups of immigrants to Shawtown. By the 1930s Russians, Poles, and Swedes joined earlier immigrants from the British Isles and Germany to work in New Castle's factories, but the largest group of twentieth-century immigrants to Shawtown came from Italy. They arrived in sufficient numbers to create an enduring Italian-American community. It is possible that some Italian Protestants came to the Dutch colony in the late 1650s as part of a group that fled to New Amsterdam to avoid persecution, but recorded names begin only in late-nineteenth-century records, as, for example, the first baptism at Saint Peter's in 1887 and the arrival of Carlo Marcozzi in 1898. Marcozzi began the migration of Italian men and families from the Teramo province of Abruzzi, a region of central Italy bordering the Adriatic Sea. For families facing hardship in a poor, mostly mountainous, agricultural area, the lure of jobs and better lives must have had a strong pull. By 1920 about 250 families from the Teramo province had chosen to settle permanently in Shawtown. Italians tended to settle in groups because of language, for most spoke in regional dialects, as did those from Abruzzi in Shawtown.

The first Italians in New Castle worked on the railroads, but soon they also found jobs as skilled, semi-skilled, and unskilled labor in the steel and fiber mills or as merchants who operated bakeries that produced the specialties of home, including pizza. Italians also became merchants with grocery stores and a cobbler's shop. Almost all of the Italians who worked were men, but two young women appear in the census as clerks in a grocery store. Tougher immigration laws after World War I slowed but did not stop Italian immigration to New Castle. Newcomers from Italy as well as from an Italian enclave in Baltimore ensured community growth.

Saint Anthony's Club on Gray Street. Originally Public School Number 3, the club acquired the building in the 1930s.

The Italians did not build their own church in New Castle because they felt welcomed at the then largely Irish-dominated, but Italian-looking Saint Peter's. They also continued their own traditions of celebrations. In the mid-

SAINT ANTHONY'S DAY FESTIVAL

For nearly ninety years, New Castle's Italian-American community has celebrated the feast of Saint Anthony on or near his birth date of June 13 with a festive event that echoes the religious traditions of their homeland. The community first marked the saint's feast day in 1924 when a band playing Italian music marched through the streets of Shawtown to rouse the residents and lead them into a day of celebration. The parade of children, then women, and finally men would stop at the convent at Fifth and Delaware streets, where the nuns would turn over the banner with the likeness of Saint Anthony that they kept under their protection throughout the year. With flags, banner, and band leading the way, the parade continued down Fifth Street to Saint Peter's Roman Catholic Church for a solemn high mass.

In 1932 a formal organization, the Saint Anthony Society, was created to carry on the annual celebration. Soon two statues pulled on decorated hand-drawn floats, one of Saint Anthony and the other of the Blessed Virgin Mary, were added to the procession. At its height the Saint Anthony's Day Celebration lasted all day, from the formal opening march through the religious services to an afternoon and evening of food, games, music, and fireworks.

The Celebration today is no longer as long or as elaborate as it used to be. The event now begins in the afternoon with the service of benediction at Saint Peter's, followed by the procession of bands, floats, and marchers, or cars for those who cannot walk the route. The carnival rides, the greased-pole climb, and the fireworks have been discontinued, but the bands playing Italian and American favorites, the homemade food, and the Italian flags hanging throughout the town, and even the ubiquitous pops of firecrackers continue as New Castle's Italian American community proudly proclaims its ethnic and religious heritage.

St. Anthony's Day parade. *(Courtesy of Alexander J. Alvini)*

1920s the Italian parishioners organized a parade in June to honor Saint Anthony, complete with statue and band music. That parade replaced an earlier parade held in October for Christopher Columbus. The Saint Anthony's Club began in 1924 and by 1936 had its own building, the old Number 3 public school on Gray Street above Tenth Street. A group of Italian Americans purchased the old school with the idea of turning it into a pasta-making facility to provide employment to those in the community hard hit by the Great Depression. When financing failed, they transformed the building into a club to provide social activities. For a time it also offered Americanization classes. In 1953 Saint Gabriele's Lodge of the Sons of Italy opened its doors at Eighth and Tremont streets. Both organizations continue to exist in a still-vibrant Italian-American community. Individuals of Italian American descent are now business and civic leaders of New Castle, but the heart of the Italian-American community remains in Shawtown, where bocce still reigns supreme.

Today Deemer Steel has been razed to the ground and replaced by the Deemer's Landing apartment complex. The only traces of early business are a few corner-cut doors that were once neighborhood stores. The Episcopal chapel, the railroad depot, and the freight station are gone, replaced by a still-developing residential pattern. Perhaps the best symbol of Shawtown old and new is the block of Gray Street between Ninth and Tenth, where a long row of older purpose-built workers' housing looks across at twenty-first-century townhouses.

New and old row houses face each other along Gray Street.

WORKERS' HOUSING SOUTH AND NORTH:
DOBBINSVILLE AND BUTTONWOOD

One of the rows of houses in Dobbinsville, built in the 1870s for workers at the Delaware Iron Company. This image dates from the 1930s. *(Courtesy of New Castle Historical Society)*

In addition to Shawtown, two communities to house workers were constructed along Route 9, rather like bookends on either side of New Castle. Today Dobbinsville to the southwest and Buttonwood to the northeast mark the limits of the town, but each began as an enclave onto itself in conjunction with riverside factories.

Dobbinsville, a five-street development, was constructed in the 1870s to provide housing for workers at the nearby Delaware Iron Company. It was named for Richard J. Dobbins, its builder, who began his career as a bricklayer in Philadelphia and rose to head one of that city's major construction firms, creating buildings large and small, from rows of small houses to prisons to major public structures. Today he is probably best known for his two major exhibition buildings done for the Centennial Exposition in Philadelphia in 1876, one of which, Memorial Hall, still stands in Fairmount Park.

Dobbinsville was a purpose-built development of over 90 two-story, two-bay brick houses arranged in five rows. As was typical in urban row housing of that era, the end

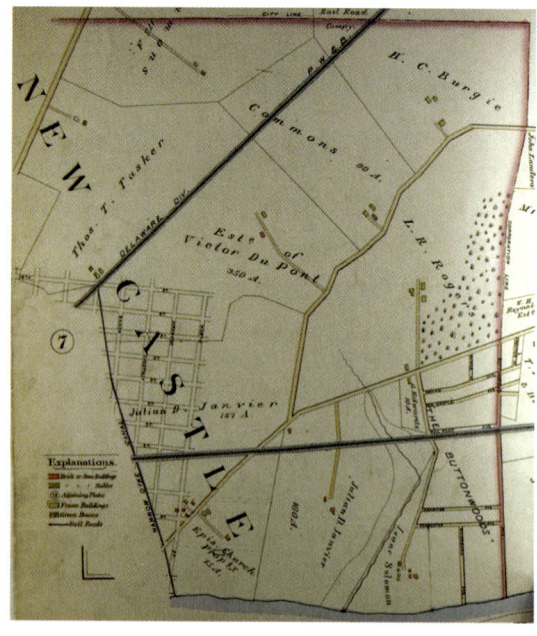

Early layout for Buttonwood, lower right, can be found in Baist's *Atlas* of 1893. *(Courtesy of University of Delaware Library, Newark, Del.)*

units were designed to accommodate businesses to serve the community, such as barbershops and grocery stores. Dobbinsville also contained three stand-alone buildings: a saloon; a bottling plant; and a church, which was subsequently moved.

Initially both workers and managers of the ironworks lived in Dobbinsville, but by the time the ironworks closed in 1899, the community had become wholly working class. Its early twentieth century residents included new immigrants from Poland and Hungary who worked in various New Castle industries. By the mid 1920s, however, much of the deteriorating enclave stood vacant. Then a New Jersey real-estate company purchased the row housing, renovated the units, and sold them on a rent-to-buy arrangement. Richard Dobbins's row houses remain today as solid, unadorned reminders of New Castle's industrial era.

Buttonwood, located to the northeast of New Castle, takes its name from its origin as a farm. The houses of Buttonwood were located near a series of factories, including early-twentieth-century steel mills that ran along the Delaware River from New Castle to South Wilmington. The location also provided easy access to the trolley line. Buttonwood was created by John H. Scott, a Philadelphia developer. In the early 1890s he had amassed a large amount of property and envisioned an enclave of more than 300 houses on lots ranging from small 100-foot plots to large tracts of six acres.

Scott's expansive dream for "The Buttonwoods," as laid out on his development plan, did not happen, but a smaller version, still called Buttonwood, took shape in the early twentieth century as an historically African-American community. In an era of racial segregation, Buttonwood offered African Americans who worked in nearby industries an opportunity to buy small, single-family frame houses.

By the 1920s, Buttonwood had grown into a lively, supportive, and largely self-contained community with its own Methodist church and

Buttonwood School, built in 1928, is now a community center.

school. The original church was replaced by its present-day successor in 1947, and the school building, constructed in 1928, is now a community center. Both continue to give Buttonwood a strong feeling of neighborhood.

SOURCES

The number of sources that provided both facts and insights for this book is so long that it could be a volume in itself, so instead we offer a listing of the materials that proved most valuable and suggestions of resources and locations for those who want to pursue additional research.

Stephen J. Cordano's selected bibliography of New Castle historical and architectural sources provides the best entry to books and articles published before 2002. His compilation, published in Constance J. Cooper's edited history of the town, cited below, is an excellent starting place for anyone who seeks to study New Castle.

Another valuable resource is electronic: the website of the New Castle Center for Historic Architecture Project (www.nc-chap.org). Created and updated by James L. Meek, this site contains a wide range of documents that include early tax lists, manuscript censuses, reprints of books and articles, oral histories, cemetery records, and much more. One caution: beware, the site is addicting.

The internet has also provided the authors with genealogical, biographical, and historical data, some so ephemeral that it perhaps would never have been found without this electronic tool. Undoubtedly the databases of tomorrow will offer even more assistance to future researchers.

Manuscript, newspaper, map, and photographic collections were treasures almost beyond imagination to us. In New Castle, the mayor's office safeguards town minute books dating to 1797, while the Trustees of the New Castle Common retain their own records. All of the town's churches have archives and web sites that include historical information. As the oldest congregations, the Episcopal and Presbyterian churches are particularly conscious of their records' value. The New Castle Historical Society and the New Castle Public Library hold some newspapers and newspaper clippings, but the most extensive collections of newspapers are held in original and microfilm forms by the University of Delaware, the Delaware Historical Society, and the Hagley Museum. The New Castle Historical Society also has a large collection of visual images as well as a priceless copy of the Latrobe town map of 1804. The other public copy of the Latrobe map, complete with text and color illustrations, is held by the Delaware Public Archives in Dover. Interestingly, the two town plans are slightly different. The three museums in New Castle, managed by the New Castle Historical Society, the Delaware Historical Society, and the State of Delaware have significant files on the history and archaeology of their sites, which they willingly make available to researchers.

Town plans, county atlases, state maps, insurance maps, road maps, soil maps, and even earlier maps that date back to the seventeenth century were invaluable resources. All of the public repositories already mentioned hold large map collections. The Sanborn fire insurance maps deserve special mention because of the level of detail they provide on the buildings of New Castle. The Delaware Historical Society holds original, colored paper copies of the insurance maps, while the University of Delaware Morris Library holds them in microfilm and digital formats.

Because this book is designed to provide an interpretive synthesis of the history and architecture of New Castle, the authors have relied more on published than on unpublished resources. Still, some important areas of study required additional research in manuscript collections. We particularly note the Delaware Historical Society's holdings of New Castle related collections such as the Kensey Johns House and Garden folder, the Julia Jefferson Collection, the typescript history of New Castle by Alexander B. Cooper, the Jeanette Eckman Collection, and the Perry, Shaw and Hepburn Collection.

The Special Collections of the Morris Library at the University of Delaware includes a collection of typescripts written and compiled by the Federal Writers' Project of the Works Progress Administration. The New Castle Historical Society's Jeanette Eckman Research Files contain copies of the deed research undertaken by Ms. Eckman that are a part of her larger collection at the Delaware Historical Society.

Books

Asbury, Francis. *Journals and Letters.* Ed. By Elmer T. Clark, J. Manning Potts and Jacob S. Payton. Nashville: Abingdon Press, 1958.

Axelrod, Alan, ed. *The Colonial Revival in America.* New York: Norton, 1985.

Bennett, George Fletcher. *Early Architecture of Delaware.* Introduction and text by Joseph L. Copeland. Wilmington: Historical Press, Inc., 1932.

Binney, Marcus. *Town Houses.* New York: Whitney Library of Design, 1998.

Biographical and Genealogical History of Delaware. Chambersburg, Pa.: J.M. Runk & Co., 1899.

Caldwell, Robert Graham. *The Penitentiary Movement in Delaware, 1776-1829.* Wilmington: Historical Society of Delaware, 1946.

Conrad, Henry C. *History of the State of Delaware.* 3 vols. Wilmington: n.p., 1908.

Cooper, Constance J., ed. *350 Years of New Castle, Delaware.* Wilmington: Cedar Tree Press for the New Castle Historical Society, 2001.

Cushing, John D., ed. *The Earliest Printed Laws of Delaware, 1704-1741.* Wilmington: Michael Glazier, Inc., 1978.

Delaware's Industries, An Historical and Industrial Review. Philadelphia: Keighton Printing House, 1891.

Eckman, Jeannette and Higgins, Anthony, eds. *New Castle on the Delaware.* New Castle: New Castle Historical Society, 1973.

Ferris, Benjamin. *A History of the Original Settlements on the Delaware . . . .* 1846. Reprint. Baltimore: Gateway Press, Inc., 1987.

Foley, Mary Mix. *The American House.* New York: Harper & Row, 1980.

Foster, Gerald. *American Houses: A Field Guide to the Architecture of the Home.* Boston: Houghton Mifflin Company, 2004.

Foster, Janet W. *The Queen Anne House, America's Victorian Vernacular.* New York: Abrams, 2006.

Fox, George. *George Fox, an Autobiography.* Introduction and notes by Rufus M. Jones. Philadelphia: Ferris & Leach, 1903.

Gibson, George H., ed. *The Collected Essays of Richard S. Rodney on Early Delaware.* Wilmington: Society of Colonial Wars in the State of Delaware, 1975.

Gilchrist, Agnes Addison. *William Strickland, Architect and Engineer, 1788-1854.* Philadelphia: University of Pennsylvania Press, 1950.

Harris, Cyril M., ed. *Illustrated Dictionary of Historic Architecture.* New York: Dover Publications, 1977.

Harris, Cyril M. *American Architecture, An Illustrated Encyclopedia.* New York: W.W. Norton & Co., 1998.

Herman, Bernard L. *Townhouse: Architecture and Material Life in the Early American City, 1750-1830.* Chapel Hill: University of North Carolina Press, 2005.

History of Firefighting in New Castle. Wilmington: Goodwill Fire Co. #1, 2007.

Hoffecker, Carol E. *Democracy in Delaware.* Wilmington: Cedar Tree Books, 2004.

Hoffecker, Carol E. *Federal Justice in the First State.* Wilmington: The Historical Society for the United States District Court for the District of Delaware, 1992.

Lancaster, Clay. *The American Bungalow, 1880-1930.* New York: Abbeville Press, 1985.

Latrobe, Benjamin Henry. *The Journals of Benjamin Henry Latrobe, 1799-1820: from Philadelphia to New Orleans.* Edited by Edward C. Carter II, John C. Van Horne, and Lee W. Formwalt. New Haven: Yale University Press for The Maryland Historical Society, 1980.

Lanier, Gabrielle and Herman, Bernard L. *Everyday Architecture of the Mid-Atlantic.* Baltimore: Johns Hopkins University Press, 1997.

Lawrence, Richard Russell and Chris, Teresa. *The Period House: Style, Detail & Decoration, 1774-1914.* London: Phoenix Illustrated, Butler & Tanner, Ltd., 1996.

Lindestrom, Peter. *Geographia Americae with An Account of the Delaware Indians.* Translated and edited by Amandus Johnson. Philadelphia: The Swedish Colonial Society, 1925.

Lunt, Dudley C. *The Farmers Bank, 1807-1957.* Philadelphia: The Farmers Bank, 1957.

Marion, John Francis. *Bicentennial City: Walking Tours of Historic Philadelphia.* Princeton: The Pyne Press, 1974.

Maynard, W. Barksdale. *Buildings of Delaware.* Charlottesville: University of Virginia Press, 2008.

McAlester, Virginia and McAlester, Lee. *A Field Guide to American Houses.* New York: Alfred A. Knopf, 2006.

McIntire, Nicholas S. *The Best of "Behind the Times": Selected Columns about New Castle.* New Castle: New Castle Historical Society, 1986.

Morgan, William. *The Abrams Guide to American House Styles.* New York: Abrams, 2004.

Munroe, John A. *Federalist Delaware.* New Brunswick: Rutgers University Press, 1954.

Munroe, John A. *Colonial Delaware.* Millwood, N.J.: KTO Press, 1978.

Penn, William. *The Papers of William Penn.* Vol. 4: *1701-1718.* Edited by Richard S. Dunn and Mary Maples Dunn, et.al. Philadelphia: University of Pennsylvania Press, 1987.

Peterson, Charles E. *The Carpenters' Company 1786 Rule Book.* Philadelphia: The Carpenters' Company of the City and County of Philadelphia, 1992.

Peterson, Charles E. *Building Early America: Contributions towards the History of a Great Industry.* Radnor, Pa.: Chilton Book Collection, 1976.

Rifkind, Carole. *A Field Guide to American Architecture.* New York: New American Library, 1980.

Rilling, Donna. *Making Houses, Crafting Capitalism: Builders in Philadelphia, 1790-1850.* Philadelphia: University of Pennsylvania Press, 2000.

Scharf, J. Thomas. *History of Delaware, 1609-1888.* 2 vols. Philadelphia: L.J. Richards & Co., 1888.

Tatman, Sandra L. and Moss, Roger W. *Biographical Dictionary of Philadelphia Architects: 1700-1930.* Boston: G.K. Hall & Co., 1985.

Tatum, Edward H., Jr., ed. *The American Journal of Ambrose Serle, Secretary to Lord Howe, 1776-1778.* San Marino, Calif.: The Huntington Library, 1940.

Tatum, George B. *Philadelphia Georgian.* Middletown, Ct.: Wesleyan University Press, 1976.

Thompson, Priscilla. *Arriving in Delaware: The Italian American Experience.* Wilmington: The History Store and Italo-Americans United, 1989.

Travers, Jim. *Images of America: New Castle.* Charleston: Arcadia Publishing, 2005.

Weslager, C.A. *The English on the Delaware: 1610-1682.* New Brunswick: Rutgers University Press, 1967.

Weslager, C.A. *The Swedes and Dutch at New Castle.* Wilmington: Middle Atlantic Press, 1987.

Wilson, W. Emerson. *Forgotten Heroes of Delaware.* Cambridge, Mass.: Deltos Publishing Co., 1969.

Zebley, Frank R. *The Churches of Delaware.* Wilmington: privately printed, 1947.

Articles and Pamphlets

Bankert, Jean E. *A History of New Castle Presbyterian Church, 1651-1989.* n.p.: 1989.

Dalleo, Bruce and Dalleo, Peter, et al. *Passing on the Story: African-Americans in New Castle.* New Castle: New Castle Historical Society, 2002.

DiSabatino, Patricia Austin. *Saint Peter's of New Castle, 1804-1984.* n.p, n.d.

Harper, Deborah Van Riper. "'The Gospel of New Castle': Historic Preservation in a Delaware Town." *Delaware History* 25 (1992-93).

Holcomb, Thomas. *Sketch of Early Ecclesiastical Affairs in New Castle, Delaware and History of Immanuel Church.* Wilmington: n.p., 1890.

Holmes, William F. "The New Castle and Frenchtown Turnpike and Railroad Company, 1809-1938." *Delaware History* 10 (1962-63).

Kruse, Albert. "An Impression of the Old Manner of Building in New Castle, Delaware." *Delaware History* 4 (1951).

Maynard, Barksdale. "New Castle's Dutch Tile House of 1687: Fraud or Genuine?" *Delaware History* 29 (2001).

Mullin, Timothy J. "A Fresh Look at Old New Castle's Architectural Heritage." *Delaware History* 32 (2007).

Spotswood, John Boswell. *An Historical Sketch of the Presbyterian Church in New Castle, Delaware.* Philadelphia: n.p., 1859.

Wolf, George A., comp. *Ideal New Castle in the State of Delaware, as it Appears in the Year 1899.* Wilmington: n.d.

New Castle Board of Trade. *New Castle, Delaware.* n.p., 1915.

Dissertations, Theses, and Reports

Anstine, Michele. "To Improve and Beautify Our Surroundings: A Study of Private and Public Gardening in New Castle, Delaware, 1880-1940." M.A. thesis, University of Delaware, 2008.

Borden, Eric J. "Booth House." Term paper, University of Delaware, 1997. Special Collections, Morris Library, University of Delaware.

Brown, Robert Frank. "Front Street, New Castle, Delaware: Architecture and Building Practices, 1687-1859." M.A. thesis, University of Delaware, 1961.

City of New Castle. "Historic Area: Guidelines and Standards Handbook." 1990.

Cooper, Constance J. "Town Among Cities: New Castle, Delaware, 1780-1840." Ph.D. dissertation, University of Delaware, 1983.

Cario, William Richard. "Anglicization in a 'Frenchified, Scotchified, Dutchified Place,' New Castle, Delaware, 1690-1750." Ph.D. dissertation, New York University, 1994.

Cottrell, Robert Curtice. "Town Planning in New Castle, Delaware, 1797-1838." M.A. thesis, University of Delaware, 1991.

Heite, Edward F. and Heite, Louise B. *Report of Phase I Archeological and Historical Investigations at the Site of Fort Casimir . . . .* Dover, Del: [Delaware Department of Transportation], 1986.

Heite, Louise B. "New Castle under the Duke of York: A Stable Community." M.A. thesis, University of Delaware, 1978.

Jennings, Leland, Jr. "The Women of Fort Delaware, 1860-1870." Term paper, n.d. Typescript file, Delaware Historical Society.

Johnson, Daniel P. "The J.T. and L.E. Eliason Company, 1868-1918: A Study in Market Transition." Term paper, 1981. Typescript file, Hagley Library.

Klee, Jeffreye. "Hidden in Plain Sight: The Old Dutch House." Historic Structures Report, 2003. New Castle Historical Society.

Klee, Jeffreye. "History of the Amstel House." Historic Structures Report, 2008. New Castle Historical Society.

"National Register of Historic Places Inventory-Nomination Form, New Castle Historic District, N-349." Prepared by Richard Jett and Valerie Cesna, 1984. State of Delaware, Bureau of Archeology and Historic Preservation.

"Recollections of New Castle, as detailed by Jos. H. Rogers, Esq., to Alexander B. Cooper . . . , September 15th, 1905." Typescript, Delaware Historical Society.

Wildes, Kristen Laham. "The Preservation of Historic New Castle: A Study in Perceptions." M.A. thesis, University of Delaware, 2003.

Williams, Susan R. "The John Wiley House, An Urban Case Study in Federal New Castle." Research paper, 1988. In possession of Robert and Joan Appleby.

INDEX